*Sonia Waterfall* 24th July 2019

# Escape to Auschwitz:

## Hulda's story

\*

by
# Sonia Waterfall

Published in 2013 by FeedARead.com Publishing – Arts Council funded

*For my parents,*
*Ilse and Sidney Waterfall*
*with thanks for the legacy they left the family.*

# Contents

# Hulda's journey, 1938 - 1944

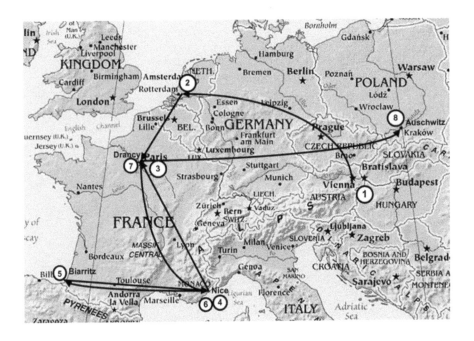

| | |
|---|---|
| 1 | Vienna |
| 2 | Rotterdam |
| 3 | Paris |
| 4 | Nice |
| 5 | Biarritz |
| 6 | Nice |
| 7 | Drancy |
| 8 | Auschwitz |

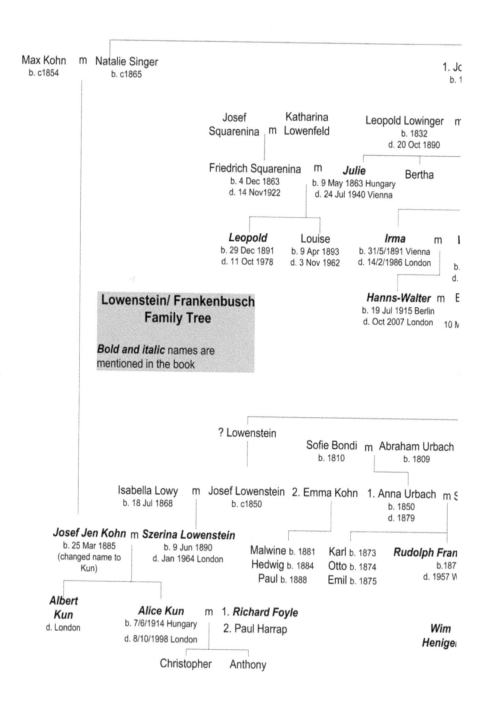

Max Kohn m Natalie Singer
b. c1854    b. c1865

1. Jc
b. 1

Josef         Katharina
Squarenina m Lowenfeld

Leopold Lowinger m
b. 1832
d. 20 Oct 1890

Friedrich Squarenina m *Julie*        Bertha
b. 4 Dec 1863       b. 9 May 1863 Hungary
d. 14 Nov1922       d. 24 Jul 1940 Vienna

**Leopold**      Louise       *Irma*       m    I
b. 29 Dec 1891   b. 9 Apr 1893   b. 31/5/1891 Vienna
d. 11 Oct 1978   d. 3 Nov 1962   d. 14/2/1986 London
                                                    b.
                                                    d.

**Lowenstein/ Frankenbusch**
**Family Tree**

*Hanns-Walter* m  E
b. 19 Jul 1915 Berlin
d. Oct 2007 London   10 N

**Bold and italic** names are
mentioned in the book

? Lowenstein

Sofie Bondi m Abraham Urbach
b. 1810       b. 1809

Isabella Lowy  m  Josef Lowenstein  2. Emma Kohn  1. Anna Urbach  m S
b. 18 Jul 1868        b. c1850                        b. 1850
                                                      d. 1879

*Josef Jen Kohn* m *Szerina Lowenstein*
b. 25 Mar 1885        b. 9 Jun 1890        Malwine b. 1881   Karl b. 1873   *Rudolph Fran*
(changed name to      d. Jan 1964 London   Hedwig b. 1884   Otto b. 1874         b.187
Kun)                                        Paul b. 1888    Emil b. 1875    d. 1957 W

*Albert*
*Kun*
d. London

*Alice Kun*  m  1. *Richard Foyle*
b. 7/6/1914 Hungary    2. Paul Harrap
d. 8/10/1998 London

*Wim*
*Henige*

Christopher    Anthony

10

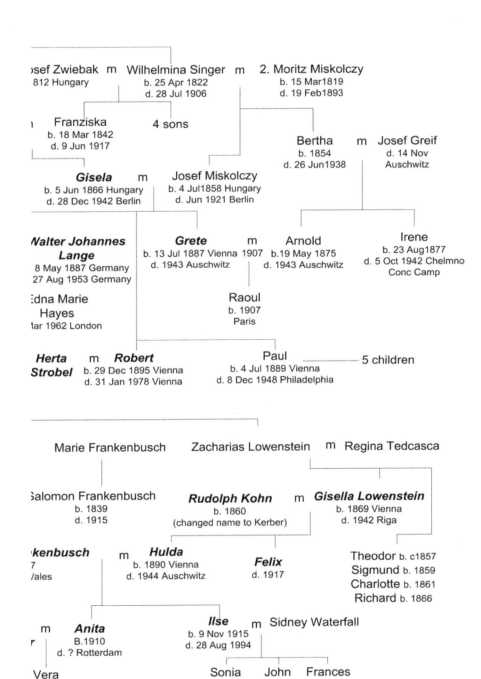

)sef Zwiebak  m  Wilhelmina Singer  m  2. Moritz Miskolczy
812 Hungary          b. 25 Apr 1822          b. 15 Mar1819
                     d. 28 Jul 1906          d. 19 Feb1893

ı    Franziska        4 sons
     b. 18 Mar 1842
     d. 9 Jun 1917                      Bertha    m   Josef Greif
                                        b. 1854          d. 14 Nov
        Gisela     m    Josef Miskolczy   d. 26 Jun1938   Auschwitz
  b. 5 Jun 1866 Hungary   b. 4 Jul1858 Hungary
  d. 28 Dec 1942 Berlin    d. Jun 1921 Berlin

Walter Johannes       Grete      m    Arnold          Irene
    Lange       b. 13 Jul 1887 Vienna 1907 b.19 May 1875   b. 23 Aug1877
8 May 1887 Germany   d. 1943 Auschwitz    d. 1943 Auschwitz  d. 5 Oct 1942 Chelmno
27 Aug 1953 Germany                                          Conc Camp

:dna Marie                    Raoul
  Hayes                       b. 1907
lar 1962 London                Paris

   Herta    m   Robert             Paul _____ 5 children
  Strobel   b. 29 Dec 1895 Vienna    b. 4 Jul 1889 Vienna
            d. 31 Jan 1978 Vienna    d. 8 Dec 1948 Philadelphia


   Marie Frankenbusch     Zacharias Lowenstein   m  Regina Tedcasca

Salomon Frankenbusch     Rudolph Kohn    m  Gisella Lowenstein
       b. 1839               b. 1860            b. 1869 Vienna
       d. 1915          (changed name to Kerber)   d. 1942 Riga

kenbusch    m    Hulda                         Theodor b. c1857
7                b. 1890 Vienna     Felix       Sigmund b. 1859
/ales            d. 1944 Auschwitz   d. 1917     Charlotte b. 1861
                                                 Richard b. 1866

   m    Anita              Ilse    m  Sidney Waterfall
r  |    B.1910          b. 9 Nov 1915
        d. ? Rotterdam   d. 28 Aug 1994

Vera                     Sonia   John   Frances

# Prologue

The story started in 2004 when my father died (ten years after my mother) and my brother and sister had to clear out his house. Amongst other items they found a cache of over 250 documents, mainly handwritten letters between my mother (Ilse), grandmother (Hulda) and great-grandmother (Gisela) that were written between 1938 and 1944 when they were separated by the events of WWII. My niece, Nicola Waterfall who had already done a lot of work on our family tree and my brother, John Waterfall who put the family tree online, sorted through the documents they found and Nicola scanned them all, saved them to disc and gave us each a copy. At this point we knew the basic details of the lives of the three women and where and when they had been born and where and when they died but as most of the letters were in German we had no idea of the intimate details of their lives. Neither my mother nor father had been willing to talk about the war years while they were alive and, to be honest, we hadn't been too interested at the time.

A couple of years later my sister, Frances Elson, visited Prague and took a day trip to Terezin (Theresienstadt) north of the capital and when I visited two years after her she encouraged me to take the same day trip. It was while I was looking round the museum there that I came across the name Riga (Latvia) and I knew that was where my great-grandmother had died in 1942 but not why she had died in that particular place when she'd lived all her life in Vienna. I discovered that many Viennese Jews had been deported to Riga to the ghettos there and later, when the ghettos became overcrowded, to camps in the area. Many Jews had been moved out of Vienna to Theresienstadt which had been used as a holding camp for some of them before they were moved on to camps further east. This was the beginning of my fascination, some say obsession, with her story and that of my mother and grandmother.

Around this time, Nicola found a translator, Gemma Kennedy, for some of the letters and around twenty of them were translated, all of them full of amazing (and sometimes heartbreaking) details of their lives during the war years. In 2009 I started writing using these translations and the many letters written in English as the basis for the first drafts of four chapters. In 2010 I decided that the rest of the letters needed to be translated before I could go any further and started on them myself with my schoolgirl knowledge of German and a good dictionary. After about five letters I realised that it would take me about ten years to complete the process and that I needed help.

I sent an email out to friends asking if they knew of anyone who might be able to help and the first person who came on board was Birgit Nielsen, a librarian from the public library in Alice Springs whom I'd known when I was working at the university library there. She had a contact in Sydney, Jochen Gutsch, who was a professional translator and also keen to help – at a price. During a brief stay in hospital in Armidale later that year, one of my nurses was Angela Lyons. Like Birgit she was also German-born, and she became interested in the project and offered her help as well. Early the following year, I happened to mention the project to an old friend in England – in fact an older pupil who had been responsible for taking me to primary school when I was five years old. She reminded me that she had majored in German at university and was fluent in the language and so Janine Hogben joined my group of translators. Over the next two years they completed the rest of the translations with a school friend from secondary school, Helen Powles, now living outside Paris, helping out with the French documents. It soon became obvious that Jochen, despite his excellent translations, was too expensive for me to continue with and Angela found that six months on she couldn't continue because of the conflict with her work and family life. However Birgit, Helen and Janine continued on and finally completed the task in early 2013.

My great-grandmother Gisela's handwriting was practically illegible but Birgit persisted with her letters until she became accustomed to Gisela's style and was able to provide a rough, if not exact, translation of the content. I will be eternally grateful to Birgit for her perseverance because from Gisela we get important details of what life was like for a Jewess in Austria once it became part of the Greater German Reich.

As the translations arrived I created, with a little help from my partner Vaina Ioane, a way of putting the documents in chronological order so that they could eventually be saved to disc so that anyone who was interested could read about the events as they happened 70 years ago.

Meanwhile, as the letters were translated, I continued writing. The 1938 and 1939 letters were the last to be translated so the first drafts of the last five chapters were written first and then I went back to the beginning of the story to write the first six chapters. The first draft of the book was completed in early May 2013. After that we three siblings proof-read, trudging through each chapter one after the other, adding and deleting, checking grammar, formatting and spelling until they were as good as we could get them. Then, once we were satisfied with the text, they were handed on to my brother-in-law, Duncan Elson who added the images, did a final edit and published.

The completed book has been a group effort and a family affair and would have been impossible for me to achieve on my own.

*

# Chapter 1
## 1938

It was 3 October, 1938 and Hulda was in Rotterdam and feeling that her life had been torn apart and that she was losing touch with her daughter Ilse, and mother Gisela, who were still in Austria.[1] She was safe for the time being but had experienced Nazi Vienna and feared for the safety of the two women left behind.

Two weeks previously the three women were living together in their apartment at *Weilburgstrasse* 4c in Baden bei Wein[2], a spa town 26km south of Vienna, waiting for Hulda's emigration papers to be finalised. Then, after weeks of waiting, everything happened very quickly and two days later she was on a train leaving Vienna and on her way to stay with Anni, her eldest daughter who had married a Dutchman, Wim Heniger, and was living in Rotterdam, where Wim's family had several menswear shops. Hulda had arrived there 10 days before on 23 September and was now trying to plan for her family's future as well as advise Gisela and Ilse from a distance about the winding up of their affairs in Baden and Vienna.[3]

\*

1938 had been a traumatic year not only for the three women but also for more than 200,000 Austrians with Jewish backgrounds.[4] Hulda herself had converted to Christianity in 1909 before her marriage and both Ilse and Anni, her daughters, had been born Protestants but Gisela had never converted and was proud of her family history and Jewish background. Of course, according to Hitler and the Nuremberg Laws, first enforced in Germany in 1935 and then introduced into those countries they annexed or invaded, all three women were considered to be Jewish. The Nuremberg Laws stated that any person who had three out of four grandparents who were Jewish, were considered themselves to be Jewish. Those with one or two Jewish grandparents were '*Mischlings*' or of mixed blood.[5]

---

[1]   Letter dated 3 October 1938 from Hulda Frankenbusch to Gisela Kerber and Ilse Frankenbusch.
[2]   Doctor's report, dated 18 August 1938 regarding Ilse's smallpox vaccination, citing this as her home address.
[3]   Letter dated 24 September 1938 from Hulda Frankenbusch to Gisela Kerber and Ilse Frankenbusch.
[4]   Encyclopaedia Judaica 1971, vol.3 col.898.
      http://www.geschicteinchronologie.ch/eu/oe/EncJud_juden-in-oe05-1938-1945-Eng. Accessed 15 February 2013.

*Nuremberg Law Chart*

\*

Hitler, himself born in Austria, had always seen Austria as being part of Germany and many Austrians agreed with him so Hitler felt empowered to bully Schuschnigg, the Austrian Chancellor, into submission. In February 1938 Hitler gave Schuschnigg a list of ten demands, including placing the country's police and internal security forces into the hands of Arthur Seyss-Inquart, a leading Nazi sympathiser, who was appointed Minister of the Interior. In return, it was expected that Hitler would acknowledge Austria's independence in a speech he was due to give at the Reichstag on 22 February.[6] This did not happen.

On 9 March Schuschnigg announced that a referendum on the issue of a free Austria would take place the following Sunday and observers predicted a two-thirds majority in favour of independence. Hitler demanded that the referendum be cancelled and that Schuschnigg should resign or German troops would invade Austria. Schuschnigg

---

5 Wikipedia. http://en.wikipedia.org/wiki/Nuremberg_Laws. Accessed 15 February 2013.

6 Singer, Peter. Pushing time away: my grandfather and the tragedy of Jewish Vienna. London, Granta Books, 2003, p.169.

could not take the risk of provoking bloodshed and resigned along with the rest of his cabinet except Seyss-Inquart.

The writing was on the wall and it was around this time that the three women decided to move from their Viennese apartment to their property in Baden. Vienna was becoming a dangerous city to live in and they believed that if they kept a low profile, Baden would be safer and allow them time to organise their futures.

Seyss-Inquart, as the sole remaining member of the Austrian government, invited Hitler to send the German army into Austria and on the night of 11/12 March Nazi troops crossed the border and Austria became a part of the Greater German Reich.[7] This action became known as the *Anschluss*.

On 15 March Hitler entered Vienna in triumph. Hundreds of thousands of waving, jubilant people lined the route of his motorcade. Tens of thousands more lived in fear and locked themselves in their homes. 'City of Frenzy and Fear' was how the *Times* aptly described Vienna that day.[8] In a later letter to Ilse, Hulda described how she felt that day - she was 'full of fear' and 'afraid of what will happen to us'. That night, she lay awake in bed, nervous and afraid but then Ilse crawled into bed with her and 'all was well again' as they drew comfort from each other.[9]

The week following the *Anschluss*, the Austrian Nazis took out their resentment on the Jews of Vienna. They plundered Jewish property and humiliated and beat up Jews. Jewish women were forced to clean pro-Schuschnigg slogans off the streets with toothbrushes and clean the toilets of the barracks used by Nazi storm-troopers. In the largely Jewish Second District, Jewish shops and apartments were looted. At the end of the week, Nazi authorities stopped the random violence and began a more systematic program of plunder and humiliation: businesses run by Jews were either boycotted or appropriated, Jewish employees in schools, banks and insurance companies were dismissed, and Jewish doctors were forbidden to treat non-Jews which meant that many were unable to make a living. Street

---

[7]   History Learning Site. Austria and 1938.
      http://www.historylearningsite.co.uk/austria_1938.htm. Accessed 13 February
      2013.
[8]   Clare, George. Last waltz in Vienna. London, Macmillan, 1981, p.220.
[9]   Letter dated 27 August 1939 from Hulda Frankenbusch to Ilse Frankenbusch.

attacks and persecution continued to be daily occurrences in the lives of Austrian Jews and in March alone 311 cases of suicide were recorded in Vienna with 267 in April.[10]

*

In May 1938 the Viennese Jewish community was allowed to renew its activities and several of its leaders were released from prison to help organise mass emigration. In August, Adolf Eichmann established a Central Office for Jewish Emigration in Vienna that was to be responsible for solving the Jewish problem – the solution was 'evict the Jews and keep as many of their assets as possible'.[11]

Vienna became the focal point for Jewish emigration from Austria. Jews seeking exit visas and other documentation necessary for emigration had to stand in long lines, night and day, in front of municipal, police and passport offices. Would-be emigrants had to pay an exit fee and to register all their immovable assets which were then confiscated concurrent with their departure from the country.[12]

With the help of the major Jewish welfare organisations in the world, the Viennese Jewish community and the Palestine Office in Vienna, thousands of Jews were helped to emigrate. Between 1938 and 1941 the American Jewish Joint Distribution Committee for Austrian Jewish Emigration alone provided close to US$2 million and lesser amounts were provided by similar organisations in other countries.

The importance of this aid grew with the increasingly distressed circumstances of Austrian Jews. Between May and July 1938 25 percent of emigrants needed financial assistance – a year later this had increased to 70 percent. Between July and September 1938 emigration reached a monthly average of 8,600. Hundreds of training courses were organised to prepare emigrants for new occupations in the countries of immigration and thousands of young people received agricultural and technical training. The community also took care of those whose education had been interrupted by their expulsion from educational institutions and of the thousands of Jews whose

---

[10]  Encyclopaedia Judaica. Op.cit. footnote 4, col.899.
[11]  Encyclopaedia Judaica. Op.cit. footnote 4, col.899.
[12]  United States Holocaust Memorial Museum. 'Vienna'. Holocaust Encyclopedia. http://www.ushmm.org/wlc/en/article/php?ModuleId=10005452. Accessed 13 February 2013.

livelihoods had been taken from them and who were in urgent need of assistance.[13]

*

Finding countries willing to accept emigrating Jews was proving a problem and President Roosevelt convened a conference at Evian, a French resort on Lake Geneva. The aim was to divide up the refugees between the attending countries so that refugees would not overburden any single country. Despite good intentions, the conference was a failure and no agreement could be reached on acceptable quotas. The US representative told delegates that existing quotas were liberal enough and the British representative said that England wasn't a country of immigration and neither were its colonies. 'Powers Slam Doors Against German Jews' was the headline in the New York *Herald Tribune* and a German newspaper said 'Jews For Sale – Who Wants Them? No one.'[14]

*

The three women in Baden made plans to leave Austria. Hulda planned to leave first as she was the one most accustomed to finding her way around in strange surroundings, spoke several European languages and hoped that the Princess Margarete Boncompagni (whom she had known since she worked for her in the 1920s) would help them once she had made contact with her. She planned to settle in France because that's where the Princess was based for six months of the year and also because she believed refugees would be more welcome there because of the French belief in '*Liberte, Egalite, Fraternite*'. Once settled she could then send for Ilse and Gisela to join her.

---

[13]  Encyclopaedia Judaica. Op.cit. footnote 4, col.899.
[14]  Baker, Nicholson. Human smoke: the beginnings of World War II, the end of civilization. N.Y., Simon & Schuster, 2008. p.89.

*Hulda Kerber 1938*

In this photo Hulda looks older than her age (48). Her hair is short, grey and slightly dishevelled and she is smiling slightly and this softens both her eyes and her mouth and reminds the viewer that she once could have been a good looking young woman.

\*

Her first letter after leaving Vienna (addressed to 'My dear Badener') implies that though she is with Anni in Rotterdam, she had made a quick trip to Paris to meet the Princess. The Princess had advised her to settle in Paris and had promised all possible support, both financially and by helping Hulda get established as a German teacher within the Princess's circle of friends and acquaintances and even to take lessons herself again. The Princess had said to her 'As long as I have money, you will have some'. Hulda sounds very relieved in her letter although she does say that she will have to make sure she stays in close contact with the Princess so she is not forgotten when the Princess is in the US where she spends six months of each year. The Princess also introduced Hulda to her bank manager, Mr Wynn, at Morgan Bank in the Place Vendome and he had promised to help organise her residence and work permits.

Her plan for Ilse, once she has managed to leave Austria, is for her to stay with Anni for a month or two because Anni has lots of work and Ilse could easily make herself useful in the kitchen and perhaps even make a bit of money for herself with her confectionary talents. But she cannot stay with Anni for more than three months because she would not be able to get a permanent residency visa unless she got a job where she is asked to stay. Hulda thinks England might be a better option for Ilse and says that it may be possible for Ilse to find a position there while she is still in Vienna. She would only stay there for 18 months, just long enough to get a residency permit, and then she could join Hulda in Paris. By that time Gisela would be with them as well and they would all be together, with Anni only five hours away in Rotterdam.

"Paris," she says, "is a city where you could live with delight – where there are hundreds of possibilities."

Hulda is full of plans for the future at this stage.

She writes about Hansi, Ilse's friend who plans to follow her when she leaves Vienna. The flies in the ointment are Roman, Ilse's fiancé, and Rudi, Hansi's fiancé who do not want to let them go.

"Be smart," says Hulda, "do not spoil your whole life – you can do much for others once you are set up yourself but not beforehand."

She says that Holland is too anti-Semitic for Hansi to go there but that it would act as a steppingstone for Ilse.[15]

*

In Hulda's next letter she is waiting to see what happens on the first of October but hopes to leave Rotterdam on the fourth. In the meantime she is going to see Gerd Jannig, a friend from Prague who is staying with his parents in law in Amsterdam and is also waiting for

---

[15] Letter dated 24 September 1938 from Hulda Frankenbusch to Gisela Kerber and Ilse Frankenbusch.

the first of October. It seemed she was planning to be in Vienna by the fifth but she writes that political developments might stop her and 'put obstacles into mine and Gerd's return journey'.

The political development she was writing about was the Czechoslovakian crisis. Czechoslovakia had been created in 1919 out of the old Austro-Hungarian Empire and was comprised of a number of different nationalities including over three million Germans who resented living under the rule of those they considered foreigners. They mainly lived in Sudetenland on the western border with Germany. In 1931 they had created the Sudeten German Peoples Party led by Konrad Heinlein and immediately demanded that Sudetenland be placed under German control. Hitler saw an opportunity here similar to the one he had acted on in Austria. As before he considered that all German people should be part of the Greater German Reich. He ordered Heinlein to start creating trouble in Sudetenland, therefore proving to the outside world that the Czech government was incapable of maintaining order in its own country. Hitler then planned to use this chaos to move his troops over the border and restore law and order.

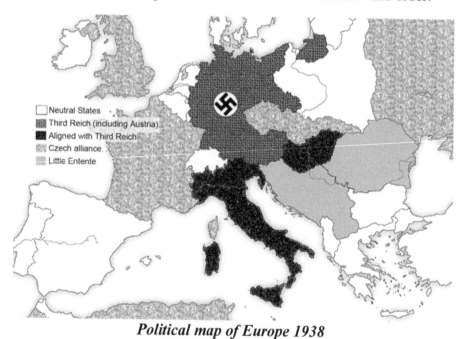

*Political map of Europe 1938*

The rest of Europe was not in a position to stop him in 1938 and it seemed reasonable that a negotiated agreement should be tried in an attempt to stop war between Czechoslovakia and Germany. Attempts to succeed started in September in Berchtesgaden at the first of three meetings that were to be held that month. Hitler demanded that the Sudetenland should be handed over to Germany. Neville Chamberlain, the British Prime Minister, agreed that those areas containing more than 50 percent Germans should be handed over to Germany and persuaded the Czechs and French to agree. On the 22 September Chamberlain flew to Bad Godesberg to meet Hitler to finalise the details of the plan. At this meeting Hitler made new demands – namely, that German troops should occupy Sudetenland and that land containing a majority of Poles and Magyars should be returned to Poland and Hungary. Britain and France rejected these demands and both countries prepared for war. At the suggestion of Mussolini a four-power conference was held at Munich to resolve the issues. Germany, France, Britain and Italy were invited – Czechoslovakia was not. The four powers agreed that Sudetenland should be given to Germany immediately and the governments of Britain and France made it clear to Czechoslovakia that if the Czechs rejected this solution they would have to fight Germany themselves. As with Austria six months earlier, the Czechs took the option of least resistance to avoid bloodshed and on 1 October 1938, Czech border guards left their posts and German troops occupied Sudetenland.[16]

*

This event created problems for Hulda. She did not know what the situation was in Czechoslovakia and her train journey took her east to Berlin and then south through Czechoslovakia to Vienna. She was worried that even if she did manage to get back to Vienna she might not be able to get out again because she was travelling on a Czechoslovak passport. She had lived in that part of the Austro-Hungarian Empire for 10 years when married to Rudolf and in 1919 when new national boundaries were put in place she realised she would now need a passport to be able to move around. According to the Nazis, Czechoslovakia no longer existed as an independent country and it was questionable that her passport might ever be recognised again within the Greater German Reich. In effect she was banned from

[16]  History learning Site. 'The Czech crisis of 1938'. http://www.historylearningsite.co.uk/czechoslovakia_1938.htm. Accessed 13 February 2013.

travelling back to either Austria or Czechoslovakia and she recognised this when she signed a letter to Ilse 'from your banned Mum'.[17]

So, she had to change her plans and decided to stay with Anni for two more weeks, before moving on to Paris. Her letter to Ilse contains a lot of business matters relating to their affairs in Vienna and who should be paid what and when. She also describes what life in Paris will be like for them once they are all living there. 'Life in Paris is very cheap' she says 'one has to allow 300 Francs per person per month for food and 400 - 600 per month for a small apartment'. 'But', she says, 'in Paris one could live!' She only wishes the issues in Baden could be resolved quickly.

"But," she writes, "when one has to leave, then one has to leave ...as long as it is possible to do so and for as long as it is necessary."[18]

*

She writes again a few days after Germany's invasion of the Sudetenland saying that what happened was predictable but she did not expect it to happen before New Year.

"Now," she says, "I am really scared that they will not let me out again once I'm in."

She has decided not to return to Baden and Gerd Jannig has also decided not to return to Prague and has terminated the contract on their apartment there. He is now financially dependent on his in-laws which, she says, 'is not ideal'. Hulda is worried that they won't be able to get their belongings out of Austria and she needs her warm clothes as winter is approaching. Ilse could bring them but Hulda doesn't think that Ilse will manage to get out of Vienna before the New Year and that will be too late. It seems that Gisela and Ilse are leaving Baden and moving back to the Viennese apartment and Hulda hopes that the move will go well. She is worried about their tax bills in Vienna and about finding a dentist in Paris – 'one who is part of our people' and asks Ilse to go and see their old dentist Dr Fleischl and see if he can recommend someone.

"Phew," she says, "all the things one has to think about!"

---

[17] Letter dated 3 October 1938 from Hulda Frankenbusch to Gisela Kerber and Ilse Frankenbusch.
[18] Letter dated 27 September 1938 from Hulda Frankenbusch to Ilse Frankenbusch.

She is also going to write to her friend, Sani, in Budapest because he has lots of contacts in Paris. She hopes that Gisela will be in Paris with her as soon as next autumn but says 'one will need a lot of patience from now on'.[19]

*

Hulda's next letter was written from the Morgan Bank Writing Room in Paris in early November 1938 and Ilse is with Anni in Rotterdam and has a job to go to in England that she obtained through an agency while still in Vienna. Once again, after weeks of queuing, filling in forms and paying fees, Ilse's papers came through suddenly and she had to leave. Saying goodbye to her grandmother and knowing that she was leaving Gisela alone in an increasingly alien Vienna was heart breaking. She was also leaving Roman, her beloved fiancé but she had to believe that they would all be together again soon and would build a new life for themselves.

She travelled with a small suitcase and a large trunk full of family heirlooms and household items. This trunk became a problem when she arrived at the Dutch border where she was told that as she wasn't a Dutch citizen she couldn't bring the trunk into the country. Using her wits, she told them that it didn't belong to her, but was part of Anni's wedding dowry. She was allowed to phone Anni who immediately realised what the problem was and told the border guards that it was hers and she'd been waiting for it to arrive, giving her address as the place where it belonged. They let Ilse and the trunk through and she travelled on to Anni's. Of course she wasn't allowed to take it out of the country again so the trunk remained with Anni throughout the war. At one point it had to be moved to a property on higher ground when there was a fear of the dykes being breached during the later stages of the war but it survived and Anni and Ilse shared the contents after the war. The trunk itself continued its journey to England and still survives though in a somewhat dilapidated condition.[20]

*

Hulda really wants Ilse to come to Paris first before she travels on to England and suggests that Ilse apply for a French entry visa immediately. As soon as she has that she would be able to get the

---

[19]    Frankenbusch, Hulda. Op.cit. footnote 16.
[20]    Letter dated 15 February 2009 from Vera Heniger to Sonia Waterfall.

Belgian visa and Hulda will send her the train ticket she needs to get her from Rotterdam to Paris.[21] The French visa took nearly three weeks to be issued and when it arrived it was only a temporary visa that would not allow her to work but she could visit for up to three months from 23 November 1938. The photo of Ilse on the document shows an attractive young woman (she was 23 years old at the time) in profile with a high forehead, straight nose and dark jaw-length hair pulled back behind her ears.[22]

*Ilse's French entry visa 1938*

---

[21] Letter dated 2 November 1938 from Hulda Frankenbusch to Ilse Frankenbusch.
[22] Republique Francaise. Recepisse de demand de Carte Didentite.no.0075. Dated 23 November 1938.

A letter from Gisela in Vienna arrived while Ilse was still in Rotterdam. Gisela writes that she is relieved to hear that Ilse has arrived at Anni's and she will be even more relieved once she knows that Ilse and Hulda are together. She writes that she is having to share the apartment with other people and that Aunt Juli has not yet moved in. Gisela has moved into Hulda's room next to the kitchen and is using Hulda's ('Mum's') furniture. Every tenant will have their own entrance to their rooms from the hallway. Roman visited her for the first time on Monday and Mrs Dillinger visits every week. Uncle Otto phoned the day before and will visit on Sunday afternoon for a chat.

But, she says, "What use is all that? You and mum are sorely missed ... I am just very, very scared. But I will make it through and imagine a better future".[23]

Gisela had every reason to be scared as Vienna had just endured a night of horror and chaos – later called *Kristallnacht* – on 9 November. The violence that erupted had been sparked off, two days earlier, by a 17-year old Polish Jew, Herschel Grynszpan, whose parents had been deported and who, in desperation, had shot a German diplomat, Ernest vom Rath, at the German embassy in Paris that morning, 7 November.[24] Hitler and Goebbels saw this as a means of demonstrating their overall strategy against the Jews. Nazis throughout the Greater German Reich were encouraged to demonstrate. In his directive to Nazi followers, Goebbels wrote 'Pull back the police. The Jews should for once feel the anger of the people'.[25] *Kristallnacht* in Vienna was particularly brutal. Nazis were joined by civilians, emboldened by the lack of police intervention, to form 'spontaneous' mobs that torched most of the city's synagogues and small prayer houses. Most of these burned down as the public and fire department stood by, intervening only when the fires threatened adjoining buildings. Jewish buildings were also vandalised and ransacked. German police arrested around 6,000 Jews in Vienna, deporting them to Dachau or Buchenwald concentration camps. Only those who were prepared to emigrate immediately, leaving their property behind, were released.[26]

---

[23]  Letter dated 4 November 1938 from Gisela Kerber to Ilse Frankenbusch.
[24]  Clare, George. Op.cit. footnote 8, p.268.
[25]  Baker, Nicholson. Op.cit. footnote 13, p.99.
[26]  United States Holocaust Memorial Museum. Op.cit. footnote 11.

Gisela, now aged 69, had survived this night of violence but had no idea what would happen next and lived in fear, hardly daring to move out of her apartment.

*

It seems that Ilse and Hulda did get to spend some time together, possibly even Christmas and New Year. Roman might have joined them for Christmas because in a later note to Ilse in 1940, he reminds her of their Christmas tree in 1938.[27] In a letter from Hulda a week after New Year in 1939, she mentions that Roman visited Gisela and handed her the money and the letter, so that means, she writes, that 'he has arrived safely' – presumably back from Paris. Ilse, meanwhile, has arrived in England and sent her mother a postcard from London. Hulda comments that she was happy to hear that the first part of Ilse's 'trip around the world' has worked out and hopes that everything has continued to go smoothly and that Ilse is now in Aberdeen.[28]

By the end of 1938, the three-woman household that had existed for nearly 15 years in Vienna, had been torn apart. The love, companionship and security that had been their life for so long, was now gone. Gisela, Hulda and Ilse were each on their own in three different countries, each having to cope with their own problems without the support they had provided for each other in the past. All of them believed that the separation was temporary and that they would be together again in the near future. Little did they know that they were never to see each other again.

---

[27]  Letter dated 26 November 1940 from Roman Rost to Ilse Frankenbusch.
[28]  Letter dated 8 January 1939 from Hulda Frankenbusch to Ilse Frankenbusch.

# Chapter 2

## Background to the story

## *Austro-Hungarian Empire 1914*

Gisela Kerber was born Gisela Lowenstein in Vienna on 11 February 1869. She was the second child of Zacharias Lowenstein and Regina Tedesca. Her elder brother, Theodor, had been born three years earlier.

The Lowensteins were a middle-class Jewish family, with an extended family spreading into Hungary and originating from Serbia.[29] Close contact was maintained between the Hungarian and Austrian branches of the family, often resulting in visits and shared family holidays.

Gisela was aged 20 when she married Rudolf Kohn, a Viennese businessman who was 17 years older than her having been born on 2 April 1852 in Mirowitz. Before he met Gisela, Rudolf had fought in the Balkan campaign of 1878-9 when the Russians were trying to extend their 'area of influence' into that area. His diary from this period of his life relates the boredom of war in those days, moving on foot from one place to another and being more concerned about where he slept and whether there were fleas or not, than about the politics and horrors of the war. When he returned from the campaign

---

[29]   Email from Christopher Foyle to Nicola Waterfall dated 12 December 2008.

he brought with him a rifle, dagger and the diary – all of which remain in the family.[30]

As was usual at that time, Gisela took with her into her new married life an extensive dowry including silverware and an immaculate set of table linen, each napkin having a beautifully executed 'GK' embroidered into one corner.[31] Both the table linen and silverware were included in the trunk transported to Holland by Ilse when she left Vienna in 1938 and so survived World War II.

A daughter, Hulda, was born in Vienna on 19 May 1890 and was followed some 4 years later by a son, Felix. Soon after Hulda's birth, a daughter, Szerena, was born on the 9 June 1890 in the Hungarian Lowenstein family to Josef and Isabella Lowenstein. The closeness in age of the two cousins brought them together and later in life their lives were to run on almost parallel lines.

Not much is known about Gisela's married life or Hulda's early years although photographs exist – mainly formal portraits or family groups.

Photo No.1 on the photo pages at the end of this chapter (pages52-53) is a lovely photo from around 1900 and shows Gisela with her two children. Hulda would have been aged ten or eleven at the time and Felix two or three years younger.

*

In the early years of the 20th century, Vienna was at the peak of its splendour as the capital of the Austro-Hungarian Empire. It was colourful and cultured. Its women set the standard for elegance in Europe and its emperor led the most glittering and glamorous court. It was the city of Lehar, Strauss and Mozart, of writers, poets and artists. For the rich there was everything, for the lower classes there were the dance halls and the Vienna Woods.[32] This was the Vienna that Hulda grew up in. The family was middle class but certainly they made the most of everything that Vienna had to offer at this moment in history.

*

---

[30] Letter from Vera Heniger to Sonia Waterfall dated 15 February 2009. Diary now in the possession of Vera Heniger.
[31] Now in the possession of Sonia Waterfall.
[32] Staples, Mary Jane. The longest winter. Bantam Press, 2009.

In 1909 Hulda converted to Christianity and a baptism certificate exists, dated 19 April 1909 and listing Rudolf Kohn as her father and Gisela Lowenstein as her mother. Hulda had already met her future husband Rudolf Frankenbusch and he converted to Christianity at the same time, much to the disgust of his Jewish family who disowned him. They married in Vienna on 30 May 1909 soon after Hulda's 19th birthday and photo No.2 on the photo pages is of Rudolf and Hulda Frankenbusch on their wedding day. Hulda added to her mother's dowry of table linen with a large linen tablecloth beautifully embroidered with 'HK' at either end.[33]

Rudolf Frankenbusch was aged 32, having been born in Prague on the 7 August 1877 to Salomon Frankenbusch, a shopkeeper, and Anna Urbach. Rudolf's mother later died in childbirth and his father remarried after her death. Rudolf trained as a chemist and by the time he was aged 30 he was managing a glass factory that produced crystal glassware, light bulbs and lamps in the rural hinterland of Czechoslovakia bordering Germany.[34] Rudolf and Hulda's first daughter, Anna Gisela Eugenie was born on 9 April 1910 at Hosena on what is now the Polish border region with eastern Germany. There is a charming photo of Gisela, Hulda and Anni (as she became known), undated but probably taken the summer of 1911 when Anni was just over a year old.

In photo no.3 on the photo pages both Gisela and Hulda are dressed in high Edwardian summer fashion in pale-coloured high-necked dresses and elaborate hats. Anni is sitting upright in her pushchair between them and is bare-armed and in a pale-coloured dress and sunhat. Both Gisela and Hulda have a protective hand on the pushchair and the fronds of a palm tree of some kind behind them indicates that it could have been a summer holiday photo.

Anni was followed five years later by Ilse Franziska Felicitas who was born on 9 November 1915 at Polaun in *Unter Polen*, a region close to the southern border of Poland and what is now the Czech Republic. Rudolf moved around a lot with his job and became well-known as a

---

[33] Now in the possession of Sonia Waterfall.
[34] Unpublished memoir of Ilse Waterfall nee Frankenbusch by Frances Elson, nee Waterfall, dated 2006.

'trouble-shooter', moving to factories where there were problems, solving those problems and then moving on to a new factory.[35]

In 1914, a daughter, Alice, had been born in Budapest to Szerina and her husband, Josef Kun[36]. It was probably because of their closeness in age that Ilse and her cousin Alice became good friends in later life.

In the meantime the Kohn family had changed their name from Kohn to the less Jewish, Kerber, in January 1912. From then on, the entire family referred to themselves as Kerber, including Hulda who listed her maiden name as that. Anti-Semitism had been around for centuries in Europe and the nineteenth century had seen it rise to the surface in small ways and undermine the glamour and the glitter of the empire.

*

On Sunday 28 June 1914, the Archduke Franz Ferdinand, heir to the Hapsburg Empire, was assassinated in Sarajevo by a young Serbian nationalist. A week later the Kaiser promised German support for Austria against Serbia. On 28 July 1914, Austria declared war on Serbia. Russia supported Serbia and on 1 August 1914 Germany declared war on Russia. On 3 August 1914 Germany declared war on France and then the following day invaded neutral Belgium. From here on former alliances were invoked, Britain declared war on Germany, and on 6 August 1914 Austria declared war on Russia. World War 1 began.[37]

Felix, Hulda's brother, who was twenty at the time, enlisted as a lieutenant in an infantry regiment and went off to fight in the Austro-Hungarian army.[38] At the same time, Josef Kun, from the Hungarian branch of the family who was a reserve officer in the same army, was called up and posted to Vienna. He took his family with him and when the war ended they stayed in Vienna, and Alice, their daughter, together with Albert their son, were both brought up as Austrians.[39]

[35] Letter from Vera Heniger to Frances Elson, nee Waterfall dated 19 March 2003.
[36] Foyle, Christopher. Op.cit. footnote 29
[37] 20th Century History. World War I.
http://history1900s.about.com/od/worldwari/p/World_War_I.htm. Accessed 12 May 2013.
[38] Letter from Vera Heniger to Sonia Waterfall 30 July 2009.
[39] Foyle, Christopher. Op.cit. footnote 29.

Photo no.4, on the photo pages is dated December 1915 and shows Felix as a handsome young man in military uniform. He is sitting on the ground with a machine gun in front of him. A second photo, dated 1916, shows him without his cap but in the same jacket. His fine features are appealing with his straight nose and full lips.

Towards the end of the war, the family received word that Felix was ill in a military hospital in Croatia and Hulda travelled via public and then troop transport to Otocal, inland from Senj in Croatia, to be with her brother and hopefully assist in his recovery. Unfortunately, after three months of suffering, he died of typhoid fever soon after she arrived[40]. By this time he had been awarded the Silver Bravery Medal and the 'Karl-Truppen' Cross. He was buried in Melinje, on what is now the coast of Montenegro, on 9 December 1918 with the hope that his remains would later be transferred back to Austria.[41] It is unknown whether this ever happened.

It was during this period as well as during an earlier conflict around 1880-1890, that the Emperor appealed to citizens to donate gold jewellery to the war effort, in return for which they would be given iron jewellery. These pieces can be identified by inscriptions on the back saying *Gold gab ich fur Eisen,* meaning 'I gave gold for iron'. Iron, noted for its strength, came to symbolise nationalism and patriotism in the struggle against the enemy.[42] Both the men and women of the Kerber family exchanged their gold for iron to help Austria. Five iron rings of varying dates and sizes remain in the family.

*

For the first 10 years of their parents' marriage, Anni and Ilse had a privileged, happy childhood, although the family moved frequently following Rudolf as he moved from one glass factory to another. After Anni's birth, the family stayed in Hosena for two more years, then moved to Teplice, a town in northern Bohemia about 46 miles NW of Prague for a further two years. In 1914 they moved to Gorlitz in the Prussian province of Silesia, on the west bank of the River Neisse about 60 kilometres east of Dresden on the Polish border. At the end of

---

[40]  Heniger, Vera. Op.cit. footnote 38.
[41]  Copy of obituary notice.
[42]  Wikipedia. http://en.wikipedia.org/wiki/Berlin_Iron_Jewellery. Accessed 28 February 2013.

1915 they moved back to what is now the Czech Republic, to Polaun, again on the Polish border. It was here that Ilse was born in November 1915 and they stayed there for four years until 1919.[43] Throughout this period however, the one element of stability in their lives was the country house that the family bought at Weisswasser, a town on the eastern boundary of Germany near the Polish border. Weisswasser was the third largest town in the Gorlitz province and during the 19th and 20th century it was the European centre of glass production.[44] For this reason, Rudolf and Hulda thought it was an excellent place to base themselves and somewhere they could always return to, Rudolf's jobs permitting. It was a beautiful spot in the lush green countryside of rural Prussia and during their times there, both girls enjoyed a happy carefree childhood. The house at Weisswasser was to stay in the family until the 1930's and remained an important influence on them despite the problems that were to arise.

A photo of the Weisswasser house, photo no.5 on the photo pages, shows a large Baroque-style house with ornamental brickwork and turrets, ivy-covered walls and trees around the brick gateposts and driveway. The women standing in the driveway, presumably servants, are all wearing knee-length or mid-calf skirts so the photo could have been taken immediately after the war or in the early 1920s.

*

Both Anni and Ilse worked hard at their school subjects and despite the age difference between the two sisters, they remained the best of friends. Their governess was Johanne Tietze whom they both loved and who was treated as one of the family. She was a young, pretty girl in her early twenties who related well with her young charges and enjoyed playing with them.[45]

This happy, carefree childhood came to an abrupt end around 1921 when Hulda discovered that her husband was having an affair with Johanne the governess who was expecting his baby. Everything changed overnight. Within weeks they had separated, eventually to

[43] Unpublished hand-written list of dates entitled 'Mein Lebenslauf' written by Rudolf Frankenbusch towards the end of his life in the 1950s.
[44] Wikipedia. http://en.wikipedia.org//wiki/Wei%C3%9Fwasser. Accessed 28 February 2013.
[45] Elson, Frances nee Waterfall. Unpublished memoir of Ilse Waterfall nee Frankenbusch dated 2006.

divorce. Anni stayed with her father and Johanne at Weisswasser and Ilse travelled with her mother, first to Italy and then to Vienna in 1923 where Gisela, by that time, was living as a widow.

Ilse and Anni were heartbroken at being separated after only six years together. Anni had waited a long time for a sister and had doted on Ilse from the start and Ilse had basked in the love of her elder sister. They both felt the loss of the other dreadfully.[46] This was the end of their life together although Ilse would go to stay with her father for a few months at a time and Anni would come to Vienna to stay with her mother. Ilse was never to forgive her father for splitting up the family and there were many years in later life when she refused to have any contact with him.

Rudolf went on to marry Johanne and they had a daughter in 1922, Johanna Ernestine Valerie Frankenbusch (or Hanne as she became known). The three girls grew up occasionally spending time together though Johanna was the only one with a really stable childhood. The photos of the girls together look staged and formal as do the family photos with Rudolf and Johanne.

Photo no.6 on the photo pages, shows, from left to right, Ilse, Hanne, Rudolf and Anni c.1925 in the garden at Wiesswasser.

*

After the divorce became final in late 1921, Hulda and Ilse moved to Fiume, where Hulda became the companion/secretary/housekeeper for the Princess Boncompagni for more than eighteen months.[47] There is a photo of Hulda and Ilse from this period of their lives and photo no.7 on the photo pages shows Hulda as a stylish young woman, seated with her face partly in shadow looking calmly and serenely at the camera and Ilse, a pretty girl, leaning into her mother and holding her hand.

Another photo of Hulda, photo no.8 on the photo pages, shows her looking carefree and happy and is the most relaxed and informal photo that has survived.

---

[46]  Heniger, Vera. Op.cit. footnote 35.
[47]  Unpublished reference written by the Princess Margarete Boncompagni, formerly Margaret Draper, for Hulda Frankenbusch. Undated.

Because the relationship with the Princess became an important one in Hulda's life – she was probably the most important person outside Hulda's immediate family – Margaret Boncompagni deserves a few words explaining her background.

Fiume[48] at this time was an independent state although it only lasted as such until 1924. After World War I and the demise of the Austro-Hungarian Empire the question of the status of Fiume became a major international problem. After two years of instability and the area changing hands between Italy and what was later to become Yugoslavia, the Treaty of Rapallo was signed in November 1920 and the Free State of Fiume was created. This continued until January 1924 when the Treaty of Rome between Italy and Yugoslavia agreed to the annexation of Fiume by Italy. After World War II it became Croatian and its name was changed to Rijeka.

Fiume had a humid subtropical climate with warm summers and mild and rainy winters. Its position at the head of the Adriatic with islands to the south and surrounded by mountains was impressive and it was no hardship for Hulda and the young Ilse to live here for two years.

Fiume's status as a free state was immediately recognised by the US, France and the UK, all of whom saw the advantage of its status and its position in the Mediterranean. Because of this, it became a drawcard for business from the three countries and a large expat community grew up. Princess Boncompagni was formerly Margaret Draper of the United States and she moved to Fiume during the breakup of her marriage. It was here that she employed Hulda as both a companion and personal assistant, dealing with the day to day business of running a large house at 17 *Via Buonarotti* and the complexities of the Princess's business dealings and personal life.[49]

Princess Boncompagni was a US citizen, and as Margaret Draper was born in 1891 just a year after Hulda and probably their closeness in age contributed to the closeness of their friendship both at this period and later in life. She had married Prince Andrea Boncompagni in 1916. Rumour has it that the elder Prince Boncompagni was short of money so he pawned a cherished tapestry to William Franklin Draper

[48] Wikipedia. http://en.wikipedia.org/wiki/Free_State_of_Fiume. Accessed 28February 2013.
[49] Boncompagni, Margarete. Op.cit. footnote 47.

who was Margaret's father, a millionaire and the American Ambassador to Italy at the time. He regretted doing this and wanted to get the tapestry back so he arranged for his son to marry the Ambassador's daughter Margaret, then aged 25.[50] When she married into the Boncompagni family she became part of a historical and influential Italian family that dated back to the 15th century and listed Popes, scholars, artists and entrepreneurs amongst their numbers.[51] It seems, however, that Prince Andrea was devoted to his mistress and their children and the marriage with Margaret was annulled in 1922, apparently never having been consummated. The cherished tapestry was returned and Margaret was allowed to continue using the name Princess Margaret Boncompagni. Meanwhile her father had died and she had inherited his huge fortune.[52]

During the period that Hulda was with her in Fiume, she was dealing with the problems resulting from the breakup of her marriage which, in a reference she wrote for Hulda, she describes as 'a difficult time' for her. Amongst other things, she says that Hulda taught her German, kept her accounts and wrote letters for her in English, French, German and Italian.

"I found her an excellent secretary," she concludes "a remarkably good teacher and a very competent housekeeper. She is most capable, businesslike and trustworthy. I have always found her very devoted and she has an excellent disposition. I left Fiume definitely [sic] and expect to establish myself in France and America. I have most pleasant memories of her."[53]

This gives us a different insight into Hulda's character – she was not just Rudolf's wronged wife or Ilse and Anni's mother. She was a talented and skilled person and was valued as such by the Princess. It also gives us some idea of the close friendship between Hulda and Margaret and explains how their lives came to be entwined during the late thirties and early forties.

*

[50]   Shorpy Historical Photo Archive. American Princess: 1922.
       http://www.shorpy.com/node/4895 . Accessed 19 April 2013.
[51]   Wikipedia. http://en.wikipedia.org/wiki/Boncompagni. Accessed 28 February 2013.
[52]   Shorpy Historical Photo Archive. Op.cit. footnote 50.
[53]   Boncompagni, Margarete. Op.cit. footnote 47.

Hulda was still based in Fiume in late 1923, making a living out of freelance writing for newspapers and magazines. There exists a letter from the Director of the *Stationes Climatica e Balneare* in Abbazia thanking her for the article she had written called 'Letter from Abbazia' that had been published in the *Neuen Freien Presse* on 8 June that year. When her father, Rudolf, died in January 1924 at the Jewish Hospital in Vienna, the Princess, who had by this time moved her household to France, sent a telegram of condolence to Hulda at Fiume. Soon after her husband's death, Gisela suggested that Hulda and Ilse should move to Vienna to join her as she was now living alone as a widow. This they did and the three generations of women were to share an apartment at *Blechturmgasse* 14/8 in the Wien IV district for the next fifteen years until the family was split up, and Gisela, the last of the family in residence, was finally forced out in 1939.

Photo no.9 on the photo pages shows the *Blechturmgasse* flat in Vienna photographed in 1999 but little changed from the building that the three women lived in during the 1920s and 30s.

The Vienna that Hulda returned to in 1924 was very different from the Vienna in which she had grown up and had known before her marriage. At the end of the First World War it had ceased to be the seat of an imperial court ruling over 55 million people, and had become the capital of a tiny landlocked country with a population of less than 7 million. Immediately after the war, the currency lost its value, there were chronic food shortages and people were dying in great numbers from malnutrition-related illnesses. By 1924 things had improved under a socialist government. 'Red Vienna' lasted until 1934. Inflation had been halted by a loan guaranteed by major foreign powers and by a switch to a new currency, the Austrian Schilling. Public housing was built and public health and education also became a priority. Vienna gained world-wide attention for its forward-thinking social programs.[54]

*

Not much is known about the family during the late twenties and early thirties. Apparently Gisela realised very soon that her husband's military pension was not going to last very long and she made the

---

[54] Singer, Peter. Pushing time away: my grandfather and the tragedy of Jewish Vienna. Granta Books, 2004. pp.129-131.

decision to invest her inheritance in a small boarding house at Baden, a spa town south of the city on the outskirts of the Vienna Woods. She hoped that this would provide an ongoing income for her small family.

It is known that Anni had her 'coming out' party in Vienna in 1928 when she was 18 years old and photo no.10 on the photo pages shows her as a beautiful young woman at this time of her life.

She finally left her father's home a year later when she was 19.[55] Soon after, in 1932, Rudolf's marriage to Johanna ended and the family get-togethers for the three girls at Weisswasser also came to an end.

Photo no. 11 on the photo pages was taken in 1932 when Ilse was 17 years old, nearly the same age as Anni in the previous photo. There are other photos of Ilse from the 1930s some taken in Budapest, surrounded by children, in 1934. Whether she was there on a visit to extended family or had been employed as a nanny is not known. Others from 1935 show her in a more rural setting.

*

In 1934, Anni met and became engaged to Wim Heniger, a Dutchman and part of a family who owned retail outlets selling clothes for gentlemen.

A letter from Hulda to Anni in July 1934 tells of Anni's engagement to Wim. She says, that from a photo that Anni had sent, Wim 'looks most serious and reliable'. She lists the household equipment that Anni will inherit as her dowry and mentions that half will be hers and the other half Ilse's, when she marries. Relations will ask her what she wants as a wedding present and Hulda gives Anni some advice:

"Tell them money," Hulda says, "so you have something in hand and can shape your home as you wish."

She says to leave the negotiations with the relatives to her.

In the same letter Hulda says that Gisela, now aged 64, had just returned from Grado (a spa town and health resort situated on a peninsula between Venice and Trieste.)[56] Hulda mentions that Gisela

[55]  Heniger, Vera. Op.cit. footnote 35.
[56]  Wikipedia. http://en.wikipedia.org/wiki/Grado,_Friuli_Venezia_Giulia. Accessed 28 February 2013.

could not stand the heat there and lost six kilos in seven weeks and did not look good. They now had to make sure that she recovered and this would be difficult with their poor food budget.

Photo no.12 on the photo pages is of Gisela taken c.1937/38 when she would have been 68 or 69. In the photo she has carefully styled short grey hair, fine deep set eyes and a determined mouth that is almost smiling which softens it a little.

Ilse, aged 19, was at this time training to become a tutor in one of the main Manicure Salons in the inner city. She had a job for a trial period of a month earning 12 schillings and was hoping that if she proved herself, then she would earn more the next month. She is working from 8am to 1pm and then 3pm to 7pm. Hulda and Gisela are not very happy about this but at least it means they can stay in Vienna and not have to start again elsewhere and take whatever job is available.

Hulda herself continues to look for a position but believes her age (44) is against her. In the meantime she continues to write short pieces for newspapers and magazines.[57]

*

A second letter from Hulda to Anni written in April 1935 mentions the number of cards of congratulations that have arrived in Vienna as well as many letters and telephone calls. The relations from Czechoslovakia had all written and Hulda enclosed 2 letters and a card that she believes Anni would find most interesting.

For the first time Roman Rost, who was to become Ilse's fiancé, is mentioned.

"He has finally become a car owner," Hulda writes, "a red and black, 2 seater DKW with a good engine."[58]

*

After their marriage, Anni and Wim travelled to Czechoslovakia so that Anni could show Wim where she was born and grew up. After that they visited the three women in Vienna. A cine film taken by Wim of a twenty-year-old Ilse ice skating in Vienna remains in the family.

---

[57]   Letter dated 2 July 1934 from Hulda Frankenbusch to Anni Frankenbusch.
[58]   Letter dated 18 April 1935 from Hulda Frankenbusch to Anni frankenbusch.

A year later, Alice Kun, aged 22, Ilse's cousin from the Hungarian branch of the family who had lived most of her life in Vienna, went to England as an English student and stayed with an English family there. That family was the Foyle family and that was how she met and married her first husband, Richard Foyle. Sometime around the time of the *Anschluss* in 1938, she managed to get her mother Szerina, her brother Albert, and her uncle Imre, out of Austria and into Britain where they spent the war years. Alice had great difficulty in getting them into the UK but through various contacts she got the help of Barnett Janner, a well known Jewish MP and it was he who helped overcome the bureaucratic resistance.[59] Her father, Josef Kun remained in Vienna at the time but spent the later years of the war in Budapest.

*

Anti-Semitism had been part of life in Europe for many years but Hitler perfected the art and introduced a more extreme form as soon as he came to power in Germany in 1933. In Austria, things had started deteriorating rapidly with the murder, in July 1934, of Engelbert Dollfuss who had seized power in February that year. Many Austrian Jews had supported Dollfuss because they believed that he was the only one who could provide the firm control needed to keep the Nazis from creating chaos and give Hitler an excuse for annexing Austria. Dollfuss sought to unite all Austrians against the Nazi threat. He outlawed anti-Semitic propaganda, protected Jewish university students from attacks by Nazi student groups and made it clear that discrimination was no longer permitted.[60]

On 25 July 1934, Austrian Nazis seized the chancellery, murdered Dollfuss and proclaimed a Nazi government. However the coup failed and the Nazis in the chancellery were shot. Mussolini moved troops to the Italian border to protect the independence of Austria. Hitler backed off from any plans he might have had for an Austrian invasion and disowned the actions of the Austrian Nazis. Dollfuss was replaced by Kurt von Schuschnigg, a member of Dollfuss's cabinet who was expected to continue his policies.[61]

---

[59] Foyle, Christopher. Op.cit. footnote 29.
[60] Singer, Peter. Pushing time away: my grandfather and the tragedy of Jewish Vienna. London, Granta Books, 2005. p.164.
[61] Ibid, footnote 60, p.164.

By 1936 anti-Semitism permeated public life in Vienna. Chancellor Schuschnigg's regime was not overtly anti-Semetic but although there was officially no discrimination against Jews, he depended heavily on various pseudo-military organisations to hold power. Some of these were, in fact, fascist militia modelled very much on similar organisations in Mussolini's Italy and had strong anti-Semetic wings.

For three years from 1935 when Schuschnigg came to power until early 1938, an uneasy calm prevailed in Austria while her neighbours south and north aligned themselves into position. Hitler, in defiance of the Treaty of Versailles sent the German army into the demilitarised Rhineland. Mussolini's conquest of Ethiopia had outraged Britain and France and this pushed him closer to Hitler. By the end of 1936, Mussolini had withdrawn his support from Austria and in 1937 he informed Schuschnigg that Italy would no longer defend Austria from attack.[62]

Meanwhile, the activities of the illegal Austrian Nazis increased, spreading fear throughout the Jewish population.

This sets the scene for Hitler's move on Austria and was the state of affairs at the beginning of 1938 when chapter 1 began. The story now continues.

---

[62]   Ibid, footnote 60, p.169.

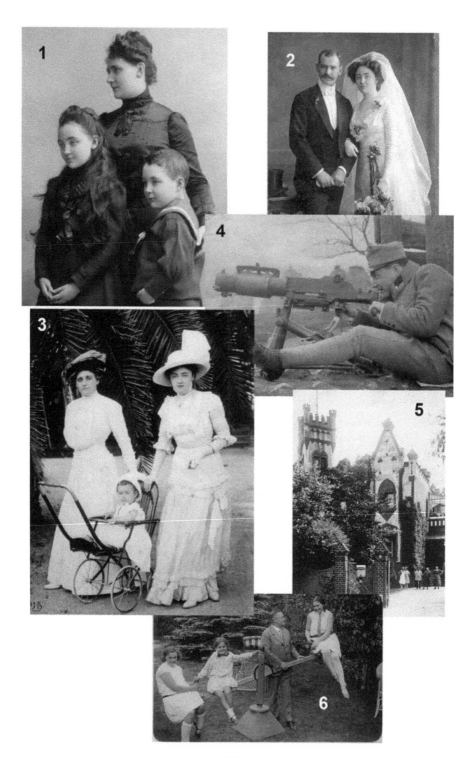

# Chapter 3

## 1939
### January
### to
### May

1939 begins with Hulda in Paris, Ilse in Aberdeen and Gisela now living alone in Nazi-occupied Vienna

Gisela is now back in the Viennese apartment at Blechturmgasse 16/8 in the Wien 4 district and is living an increasingly isolated existence. There is nowhere for her to go nowadays as many of her friends and extended family have left and those remaining are mainly elderly, living in fear and keeping a low profile. She cannot go to a cafe or sit on a public bench in a park any longer – the benches in the nearest park have *Juden Verboten* stencilled on them. She cannot walk in the Prater as she, Hulda and Ilse used to do, she cannot go to a bookshop or hair salon. She dare not take a tram as she has heard of Jews and those who look Jewish being thrown off. She cannot go to a cinema, nor to the Opera and even if she could, she would not hear music written by Jews, played by Jews or sung by Jews. Opera has been Aryanised. There are stormtroopers stationed at the end of the train line at Neuwaldegg to prevent Jews strolling in the Vienna Woods.[63] She is dependent on friends phoning or visiting her for any social interaction. She is living in one room of the apartment that the three women had shared comfortably for 15 years and, aged 68, she is having to look after herself and share the apartment with other people, most of them strangers.

\*

Ilse is working for a family in a village near Aberdeen in the northeast of Scotland. Mrs Clark, her employer lives on Dalmuinzie Road in Murtle, a small settlement about 20 miles southwest of Aberdeen on the A93. It is a rural, wooded area. Mrs Clark sounds to be a kind person and a fair employer, who nevertheless expects her staff to work for their salaries. Ilse has her own room and 'all amenities' and the work is not too hard.[64] The train trip from London to Aberdeen had taken a whole day and she had changed trains in Edinburgh and arrived in Aberdeen late that night. Mrs Clark had met the train on its arrival at Waterloo Station in Aberdeen and had taken Ilse back to her new home in the country. Despite being surrounded by kind people, Ilse is desperately lonely and missing Hulda, Gisela and

---

[63]   De Waal, Edmund. The hare with amber eyes: a hidden inheritance. London, Vintage Books, 2011, p.261-262.

[64]   Letter dated 11 January 1939 from Hulda Frankenbusch to Ilse Frankenbusch.

Roman. However she is relieved to be out of Vienna and in a free country where the people do not care whether she is Jewish or not and where there is no chance of jackbooted brown- or black-uniformed men stopping her in the street and asking to see her ID. She knows she has to make the most of the opportunity she has been given. In London she had immediately been aware of being in a different country. The tangy smoky foggy air of pre-war London and the row upon row of little houses all looking alike would always be symbols of freedom for her. The countryside in Scotland seemed more familiar despite the weather.

\*

*Hotel de Palais Bourbon.*
*Hulda lived here for 12 months from October 1938*

Hulda is in Paris, living at the *Hotel de Palais Bourgogne, 49 Rue de Bourgogne*, and despite being alone seems to be enjoying the city. She writes that she is spending a lot of time with Sani (Alexander

Torday, a friend from Budapest) and they usually have their meals together. She is writing her postcard at 'Weber's' and tomorrow she is going to 'Recht's' with Robert (Robert Miskolczy, a distant cousin from Vienna) then to a German lecture with Sani. She sounds to have a full social life. She has heard from Else Kriknelt, who's daughter, Liesel, is in London. Her other daughter, Gretl, will follow and Else herself will start work there soon.

'Then,' says Hulda, 'it's my turn! Long live England'.

So it seems that her plans have changed and she is now hoping to join Ilse in Britain. Hulda's cousin, Szerena Kun, has also written from London and she is working in an office there.[65]

\*

Hulda's next letter tells Ilse that she has submitted the visa application for Gisela and can't wait to hear back from them. She says that everything is the same in Paris. Sani still cracks bad jokes and his caricatures are even worse. Mrs Recht is homesick and Mr Recht still stops at every food stall he passes. Every Monday she meets with the German writers group and enjoys 'the different crowd'. She works with Sani, translating for him, but he never has enough time – he is always out socialising and then sleeping in. She tells Ilse about a letter she has had from Aunt Szerina in London who says

"Ilse shouldn't take it too bad if she doesn't like it where she is, we can always get her another position in case it is necessary"

Hulda gives Ilse a contact address in case she should need it: Szerina Kun, c/o Bourne & Hollingworth Ltd, Oxford Street, London W.1.[66]

\*

At the end of January, Hulda is feeling sorry for Ilse being on her own but says that things will change once Hansi (Ilse's best friend) arrives. Hulda has received a 'very, very lovely letter from Roman' which she is quite delighted with. He has asked Hulda to send some warm pyjamas from him to Ilse which she will do tomorrow. Two

---

[65]   Letter dated 8 January 1939 from Hulda Frankenbusch to Ilse Frankenbusch.

[66]   Letter dated 11 January 1939 from Hulda Frankenbusch to Ilse Frankenbusch.

days ago she'd heard rumours about riots in Austria and is worried because she hasn't heard from Gisela for some time. She asks Ilse to be sure to write to Gisela in Vienna.[67]

*

Hulda's next letter written only four days later, tells Ilse that she benefits from the fact that today is the last day of the month. This means that Hulda has only two Francs in her pocket so can't even go to a cafe so she has plenty of time to write a long and detailed letter. Anni has forwarded a letter from 'Dad' saying he also wants to leave and asking if Hulda can do anything about it.

"So" she says, "I'm supposed to look after that on top of everything else. You can totally forget about that" she says.

The bitterness from the break-up of their marriage obviously remains.

Ilse has apparently written to Hulda about Hansi changing her plans. Hulda is disgusted with Hansi's unreliability.

"Now you can see what she is like!" Hulda says vehemently, "You have adjusted your plans so they suit her, didn't want to do anything without her despite being told that you shouldn't make yourself dependent on her, and now, at the first opportunity, when you have counted on her and need her help, she lets you down!"

She tells Ilse not to do anything stupid because of Hansi.

"Because," she says, "Your position, the decent people you works for and your flat are not to be sneezed at."

Hulda asks how Ilse's English is coming along and advises her to 'industriously read the newspapers' for practice. Ilse has to make sure that her English is perfect as Roman is investigating going to America. He has received a very nice letter from Gellert in America (Roman has been working for Gellert, a branch of Westinghouse, for five years in Vienna) and they have offered help with finding a position, obtaining residence permits etc once Roman is over there.

Hulda comments "the idea looks promising".

---

[67]   Letter dated 25 January 1939 from Hulda Frankenbusch to Ilse Frankenbusch.

She has had a good time with Sani and last week he took her to a Chinese restaurant in the Latin Quarter for a farewell meal. Sani ate with chopsticks but 'your mother decided to use a good European fork after five minutes'. Now Sani has gone off to Zurich to meet his father and Hulda is on her own again.[68]

*

In February Hulda seems mainly to be concerned with her teeth – she has to have root canal work done on five of them. She went to the *Hospital Peletier* and found a dentist from Vienna, Dr Meslier. She also said that the head physician and the head psychiatrist are also refugees from Vienna. So far she has had one root pulled and is on painkillers which are making her feel a bit dizzy. She also needs two new crowns and the 'two ugly front teeth in the middle' will be pulled out and she'll get 'a whole new piece' to replace them. The whole lot will cost 1500 Francs to be paid in monthly instalments of 200 Frs. It seems that Ilse is suffering from the cold in Aberdeen because Hulda tells her that spring has come already to Paris but that she can't enjoy it properly because of the teeth.[69]

*

From her next letter it seems that Hansi is definitely not joining Ilse in Aberdeen and Ilse is complaining about not having enough free time. Hulda quotes a friend who has written from England who says:

"Ilse should not be content with no free time. She has the right to have a free afternoon every week and the same every second Sunday."

Hulda advises that Ilse says something to Mrs Clark, otherwise she won't last the distance.

She tells Ilse that Gisela is very unhappy and that she (Hulda) has no idea how to speed up the visa application.

"Because of the thousands and thousands of refugees who have now returned from Spain," Hulda complains, "all the departments are so overloaded that everything is taking so much longer".

---

[68]   Letter dated 31 January 1939 from Hulda Frankenbusch to Ilse Frankenbusch.

[69]   Letter dated 12 February 1939 from Hulda Frankenbusch to Ilse Frankenbusch.

The Spanish Civil War had ended and on February 27$^{th}$ the United Kingdom and France recognised Franco's government. A month later Franco assumed power in Madrid.[70]

Back in mid February, Hulda's temporary visa has only been extended for two months and she is still waiting for her French ID card.

She tells Ilse about a family they know, the Grimeissens, who emigrated to Brazil. They are having a tough time over there. Hulda and other friends in Paris have written to them advising them not to try and return to Europe but to move to a better climate in Brazil.

"Brazil is large enough", she writes, "and the surrounding areas of Rio are supposed to have a notably good, healthy climate."

She ends by saying that Sani got a bad dose of flu in Switzerland and had to spend two weeks in hospital there which meant he has had to delay his return to Paris.[71]

*

In her next letter at the end of February, Hulda is obviously trying to persuade Ilse not to be rash and move away from Aberdeen.

"It is lucky that you are in the countryside and not in a big city" she writes, "as it's well known that girls who work in provincial households are treated well and humanely...while those who work in the cities are exploited, have to work late nights and are never able to get by on their wages because there are more opportunities to spend their money".

She also says that now, with summer coming, "if I lived near the sea, then wild horses wouldn't drag me away".

She has had good news about Gisela's visa application and has been told that it could still take another two or three weeks but that it will most likely be granted. She wrote immediately to Gisela to give her some hope for the future. Meanwhile, newspapers are reporting that all gold and silver still owned by Jewish people has to be surrendered and Hulda wonders if Gisela will manage to avoid this. Luckily, Ilse's silver is with Roman and because the law speaks explicitly of 'Jewish

---

[70]  Wikipedia.http://en.wikipedia.org/wiki/1939 .Accessed 3 March 2013.

[71]  Letter dated 19 February 1939 from Hulda Frankenbusch to Ilse Frankenbusch.

people with German citizenship', maybe Gisela could say that the remaining silver that she has, was in fact Ilse's because of Ilse's Czech citizenship. She suggests that Ilse writes to Roman about it but she must be careful how she puts it because of the censorship.

She tells Ilse that Sani is back, he is living again in his old room at the hotel and invited Hulda out for a welcome back meal at the Chinese restaurant. He wants her to work with him translating his second novel and will pay her, which, she says, 'would be very nice'.[72]

*

Hulda's next letter at the beginning of March tells Ilse that Robert was threatened with deportation because he told the authorities he was living outside Paris when, in fact, he was living in the city. His sister had to intervene and now he has to live outside and is only allowed into Paris for a few hours each week. His wife is still not with him and it doesn't look as if she'll get her visa in the near future.

Hulda has also heard some sad news from Vienna. Her friend Rosl Schwarz, who had stayed in Vienna to take care of her 78 year old mother, wrote to Hulda to tell her that her (Rosl's) brother, who fled six weeks ago with his wife and two children to Palestine, has died there of typhus.

"Isn't that horrible," exclaims Hulda.[73]

For the next few months there is a lot of discussion about where Roman and Ilse will ultimately settle. Roman is considering Yugoslavia and opening his own business there but Hulda thinks America is a better option particularly because he has a contact there and Gellert has offered him all possible support. However, as she says, this is ultimately Roman and Ilse's decision.

In one of her letters in March, she gives Ilse news about Irma and Walter Langes. She says they will have to get divorced 'because of the specific wish of Goering!', presumably because Irma is Jewish and Walter is Aryan. This is only a 'pretend' divorce and Irma hopes to get a visa to come to Paris for some time while Walter will stay in Berlin and try and liquidate his business or sell it.

---

[72]   Letter dated 26 February 1939 from Hulda Frankenbusch to Ilse Frankenbusch.

[73]   Letter dated 3 March 1939 from Hulda Frankenbusch to Ilse Frankenbusch.

"But then," says Hulda, "there are still the houses in Berlin and the estate in Rahnsdorf! They have money in England and they want to stay in England or maybe even emigrate to Australia."

The Langes are supporting Gisela in Vienna with 120 RM [*Reich Marks*] every month while Hulda puts aside the equivalent amount in Francs for Irma when she arrives. 'This is clever, isn't it?' says Hulda. And yes, it is, because this way they both avoid having to send money between different countries with all the red tape involved in doing so. The Langes' money is just moved within the *Reich* – from Berlin to Vienna.

'Isn't it terrible how families are torn apart and wealth destroyed,' says Hulda, probably thinking about her own family as well as the Langes. Walter Lange has recently equipped the entire Berliner 'Hof' with fur coats and made a fortune again!

"But what use is it to him now," comments Hulda.[74]

*

Meanwhile on 15 March 1939 Nazi troops moved out of Sudetanland, into Czechoslovakia and occupied Prague. Two days later Neville Chamberlain makes a speech in Birmingham stating that Britain will oppose any effort at world domination on the part of Germany. The first Anderson shelters have already been built in London. Europe is slowly but surely moving towards war.[75]

*

In her next letter Hulda is devastated by the news about Czechoslovakia.

"What about our relatives in Prague, Brunn, Pilsen, Mirovie," she says, "and also Ilba and Aranka in Slovakia - no one is spared. Think of the old Frankenbusch shop in Prague – I can't bear thinking about it!"

She is worried about Gisela who is having to cope with this bad news all alone. She wonders what will happen to their papers and passports now. The *Paris-Soir* has reported that Benes in Chicago is the head of a 'provisional Czech government' and will have

---

[74] Letter dated 12 March 1939 from Hulda Frankenbusch to Ilse Frankenbusch.

[75] Wikipedia. Op.cit. footnote 70.

representatives in all Czech consulates who will look after the concerns of 'Czech citizens living abroad'. This would not be too bad for them but they will have to wait and see if it is true.

The Czech travel agency in Paris is displaying a black beribboned casket and people are queuing to lay flowers at the 'grave of Czechoslovakia'. The worst part of all this for Hulda is that there is a whole new stream of emigrants entering France which means that the departments will be even more overloaded and Gisela's permit will be delayed again. Hulda is very anxious and says she'll continue that way until her mother is with her in Paris.

She has just received a letter from Ilse and is glad to hear that Hansi has arrived and is now working with Ilse. 'Hopefully', Hulda says, 'she'll be able to cope with the work'. She comments that it is well known that Jewish girls are not good at housework and Hansi is just typical.

"But," she says, "we will hope for the best."

She tells Ilse that the refugee community in Paris is very nervous after the latest developments. Sani doesn't know what to do. Something is developing in Hungary and he still wants to go for a few weeks to Budapest to get his belongings. His father, apparently, packed his suitcase weeks ago and has money ready to leave immediately if something goes wrong. He will flee over the border in a private airplane.

"One fears the worst for Hungary", says Hulda.[76]

*

Something *was* brewing in Hungary – on 23 March 1939 the Slovak-Hungarian War began and ended two weeks later with Slovakia ceding eastern territories to Hungary.[77]

At the beginning of April, Hulda reminds Ilse that it is Anni's birthday on the 9th and says she is thoroughly fed up with Paris. She would love to go to somewhere like Nice where she could lie down and sunbathe properly. She says she always gets 'that *Wanderlust*'

---

[76] Letter dated 19 March 1939 from Hulda Frankenbusch to Ilse Frankenbusch.

[77] Wikipedia. Op.cit. footnote 70.

when spring comes but knows that she has to bide her time until Gisela is with her.

"Anyhow," she says, "I don't envisage ending my days in Paris. I am already too tired of the endless hurly-burly!"[78]

*

The next letter to Ilse was written just after Easter and Hulda said it was a sad Easter spent on her own but the weather was glorious. She says that Paris is flooded with foreigners and it's impossible to move on the boulevards or get a seat in a cafe, cinema, theatre or variety club – everything is sold out weeks in advance. She went for a walk in the *Bois de Boulogne* but it was crowded with people and she had to pay five francs for a cup of coffee. To make up for that she walked all the way back along the *Champs Elysee* to the *Place de la Concorde* and then over *La Concorde* Bridge to the hotel. She remembered that once the two of them had walked the same way together. Then she got afraid and anxious again and it was only writing the letter that made her feel better.

She is terribly on edge about Gisela and has been told that the visa application is proceeding and that Gisela will be notified by the consulate in Vienna in due course so there is nothing more that Hulda can do from Paris. She is very afraid that communications are breaking down between Germany and France and that Gisela will never be able to leave Vienna.

"What then?" she asks, "It doesn't bear thinking about at all!"[79]

*

By mid April Hulda is worried about Anni because she hasn't heard from her for over three weeks. The Paris newspapers are writing about the call-up of reservists, the mobilisation of troops, the preparation of defences in time of flooding and the blowing up of bridges in Holland.

"Things really look bad in my lovely Europe," says Hulda.[80]

---

[78] Letter dated 2 April 1939 from Hulda Frankenbusch to Ilse Frankenbusch.

[79] Letter dated 9 April 1939 from Hulda Frankenbusch to Ilse Frankenbusch.

[80] Letter dated 16 April 1939 from Hulda Frankenbusch to Ilse Frankenbusch.

*Hulda's letter to Ilse 16 April 1930*

*

Everywhere, preparations are being made for war and nations are aligning themselves on one side or the other. At the end of March, Britain had pledged support for Poland in the event of an invasion. Ten days later the Women's Royal Naval service was re-established, closely followed by the Military Training Act, introducing conscription, which was passed and would come into force early in June. From 3 June 1939 all British men aged 20 and 21 would have to undertake six months military training. Italy had invaded Albania and Hungary had left the League of Nations. At the end of April in a speech in the *Reichstag*, Hitler renounces the Anglo-German Naval Agreement and the German-Polish Non-Agression Pact.[81] Europe was in turmoil.

*

Hulda advises Ilse to stay in Scotland because London will be in as much danger as Paris. She says the atmosphere in Paris is gloomy with gas masks and sand bags being distributed and the Metro stations being converted into bombproof shelters. She has at last received her French identity card and it has been made out for three years duration.

---

[81]  Wikipedia. Op.cit. footnote 70.

It is back-dated to 15 October 1938 which means she can apply for a work permit 'this coming October'.

*Hulda's French ID card*

The bad news is that she was called back to the Ministry about Gisela's visa application and was told that 'as a consequence of international complications entry into the country is blocked!' This was exactly what Hulda had feared and after being told this, she was in tears and was advised to write a special request to the Minister himself. Sani is going to help her write this and she will take it there tomorrow, 'but', she says, 'Grandmother must not learn a word of this' as it will destroy her morale.[82]

*

It is around this time that Ilse writes an impassioned plea to Westinghouse in America, trying to find a position for Roman saying that he is unable to write himself as all letters leaving the *Reich* are censored. At the same time she is also investigating the possibility of her and Roman emigrating to Brazil and writes to the Brazilian Consulate in London enquiring about visas and other documents she might need. She says she has a residency permit in England and an invitation from a friend in Rio.[83] Ilse is getting desperate to find somewhere that she and Roman can be together.

Hulda's next letter at the end of April tells us that Roman is unable to get a visa to come to England and Ilse is very unhappy. But Hulda says that she never expected him to be able to get a visa and she's relieved that he isn't coming to England as he would have run the risk of being arrested as a spy on his arrival. All anti-German countries are obsessed with the idea of spies entering the country. She says that in Paris no refugee dares to go to a night club because they are raided regularly and the slightest bit of stupid behaviour can arouse suspicions. So there would have been a lot of suspicion about why a German Aryan would want to come to England. As long as the present circumstances continue there is no chance of Roman getting a visitor visa.

Hulda continues by telling Ilse about the new swimming pool that is being built at *La Concorde* Bridge, quite close to her hotel. She tells Ilse that it is twice the size of the one at the *Aspern* Bridge in Vienna. Not that she can think of swimming yet because, after a few nice days, it's turned cool again and she's writing her letter in bed to keep warm. She has her vases filled with lilac tho as the markets are full of them and several sprays only cost a few cents. She is still very much on her own and quite often, after having breakfast with Sani, she doesn't talk to anyone else all day.[84]

---

82  Frankenbusch, Hulda. Op.cit. footnote 80.

83  Undated letters from Ilse Frankenbusch to Westinghouse and the Brazilian Consulate.

In another letter Hulda says it is bliss that Anni, Ilse and herself are all able to live in friendly countries.

"Although," she says, "one can never be sure with Holland what can happen next!"

She just wishes that Gisela could be with them. Gisela has given notice on her apartment believing that she'll be leaving soon. So she has to be out by the 1 August and Hulda worries that if she can't leave Austria by then, what will happen to her.

She tells Ilse that she and Hansi should not be too unhappy. They haven't been separated from their men for very long and Hulda knows several young women who have been in Paris alone for over a year while their men are in Dachau or some other camp. Hulda tells the girls to remember that they are in a better situation than thousands of others and then ends by saying that she'll stop sermonising now.[85]

*

In the next letter a week later, Hulda mentions Ilse's father and says he is travelling via Rotterdam to Birmingham where, it seems, he has obtained a position. Ilse is already talking about moving to Birmingham to help him run the business and this has hurt Hulda as she feels she would lose Ilse if this happens. She admits though that Ilse might be happier running the business for her father than cooking for strangers. But, she says, it might never happen so why worry about it at this stage.

Hulda's teeth come to the fore again and she says she has signed a contract with a new dentist – a Dr. Altmann, also from Vienna, which will save her 450 Francs. She paid the deposit after selling some Marks when she got 60 Francs for 4 Marks.

"That is better than gold," she says, "although selling Marks is becoming more difficult because those interested in buying are becoming harder to find."

That day, Sunday, she had been to the zoo in Vincennes despite the miserable weather. She says the zoo wasn't as good as the one in the

---

[84]  Letter dated 23 April 1939 from Hulda Frankenbusch to Ilse Frankenbusch.

[85]  Letter dated 30 April 1939 from Hulda Frankenbusch to Ilse Frankenbusch.

*Bois de Boulogne* but the castle and park at Vincennes are 'truly lovely'[86]

*

A note from Gisela to Ilse calls her 'you golden girl' and says that her letter made her very happy. Gisela asks if the flowers and dirndl have arrived. It sounds as if she is regretting giving notice on the apartment and wonders if she did it 'too soon'.[87]

The next letter in mid April is all about a collection of photos that have arrived from Vienna and which Hulda is forwarding on to Ilse. She hints that if Ilse were to have an enlargement made for her mother's birthday that would make her very happy. Hulda tells Ilse which ones she prefers including two where she's wearing a hat.

"But," she says, "if at all possible one should immortalise oneself without a hat."

She cannot resist making a typical motherly comment:

"You are shown off to the best advantage in the profile photos. The reason being that one sees only a little of your high forehead. For, if one may ask, why do you once again have a hair style that does not do you justice? ... Please try and improve yourself," she says.

Ilse has obviously enclosed a letter to Robert because Hulda says she'll send it on to him as she hardly ever sees him now because he lives outside Paris at Lagny. Though she says she might visit him over the Whit weekend.

Hulda writes that the whole of Paris is busy with festivals at the moment. There's the Festival of the Revolution, the Joan of Arc Festival, the Trade Fair, the Arts and Crafts Exhibition and, last but not least, close to the hotel, at the *Esplanade des Invalides* is the *Fete des Invalides*. The latter is a huge fun fair where the noise goes on well into the night. There are at least twenty merry-go-rounds, three huge circus tents, around twenty shooting galleries, just as many food stalls and lots of other attractions. That started yesterday and goes on for fourteen days!

"It's impossible to sleep with the windows open," complains Hulda.

---

[86]  Letter dated 7 May 1939 from Hulda Frankenbusch to Ilse Frankenbusch.

[87]  Letter dated 12 May 1939 from Gisela Kerber to Ilse Frankenbusch.

She tells Ilse how she had met Herr and Frau Baruch whom they had known in Vienna. Amongst other things they told her that Gisela would probably get her pension again in Paris as all the money from Vienna was transferred to London and the two secretaries who fled Vienna are now in London and being paid to administer the funds. She comments also that when Gisela arrives 'she will find a circle of friends and acquaintances' in Paris 'such as she could only wish for'. She ends with news about other people she has met that they both know.[88]

*

Hulda and Ilse are exchanging photos and in her next letter Hulda encloses the one of herself. She says it is 'frightfully touched up'. She says that the photographer has given her a beautiful classical nose – 'where is my hump?' she asks. Also a perfect mouth unlike her natural one and eyelashes like a film diva. She has been left with her 'sweet little mole' on her right cheek, which, she says was 'nice of them'.

Ilse and Hansi are obviously still planning their onward travel with their men because Hulda writes about Roman, as an engineer, being able to find work in America immediately and suggests that he should take advantage of the fact that the World Exhibition is on over there and get a ticket to go there. Ilse could always follow him there later. Unfortunately Roman is still talking about Brazil which Hulda finds 'nonsensical' as she has heard that there are no prospects there for anyone who doesn't speak the language. Ilse seems to have asked if Hulda could help her financially if she and Roman moved overseas but Hulda says that Gisela's move will strain her finances and once again she'll be up to her ears in debt.

Her birthday had been two days earlier and she spent most of the day alone except for a meal out with Sani in the evening where she treated herself to asparagus and a peach melba. The day before her birthday she 'got crowned with a golden crown' [her new tooth] and today, Sunday, she went 'on a glorious excursion to St. Cloud.'

"That," she says, "is the nicest thing I've seen so far in Paris – similar to our *Schwarnenberg* Park in *Neuwaldegg* – but much, much bigger."

---

[88] Letter dated 14 May 1939 from Hulda Frankenbusch to Ilse Frankenbusch.

It reminded her very much of the Vienna Woods and she says she'll probably go there again at Whitsuntide.[89]

\*

A brief note from Gisela tells Ilse that Roman brought her a box of chocolates for Mothers Day and stayed with her listening to her problems until 11.45pm.[90]In a city where there were risks for non-Jewish people being associated with Jews, Roman is defying the prevalent anti-Semitism of the time. He was in danger of coming under political suspicion and becoming known as a pro-Jew sympathiser. His visits to Gisela and his generosity with the time he spent with her would have meant a lot to her simply because he was Aryan. The gifts and food parcels he brought would have provided, not only physical sustenance, but also moral support during these uncertain times.[91]

\*

Hulda next writes to Ilse on Whitsunday which she has spent with Sani at the Paris Trade Fair which, she says, is 'much more magnificent than the one in Vienna but definitely not so tasteful – as always in Paris, nothing but a big funfair'. Sani, of course, is back in Paris but not living in the same hotel as her any longer but on the other side of *Les Invalides* so still quite near.

She has been working hard on Ilse's behalf but has not been able to find out much because each Brazilian consulate has different rules for granting visas and what might be granted in Paris, might not be granted in London. So, she says, Ilse will have to find things out for herself in London. Hulda says that she cannot intercede any further on Ilse's behalf until Gisela is with her and has her permit to stay. When she applied for Gisela's visa, the authorities specifically asked about Ilse and whether Hulda was supporting her as her income is enough to support two people but not three. So, she writes, she cannot do any more until 'Grandmother's affair is sorted'. All she can do is preach patience – 'patience, patience and again patience!' She tells Ilse not to get depressed and that things can only get better.

---

[89]  Letter dated 21 May 1939 from Hulda Frankenbusch to Ilse Frankenbusch.

[90]  Letter dated 23 May 1939 from Gisela Kerber to Ilse Frankenbusch.

[91]  Singer, Peter. Pushing time away: my grandfather and the tragedy of Jewish Vienna. London, Granta Publications, 2003. p. 196-198.

Hulda tells Ilse that Robert and Hertha Miskolczy have got a job together in England at a rectory. They got the positions in answer to an advertisement in The Times – Hertha as a cook and Robert as a servant. At the moment Robert is on an agricultural retraining course while he waits for his permit to come through.

Anni wrote a long letter with Hulda's birthday parcel and said that her father was still with her waiting for his English visa. Anni is worried about her father because she says he is looking his age and getting a bit doddery and she wonders whether he will still be able to do the work when he starts his new job in England. Hulda comments that it would probably be a good idea if he stayed a bit longer with Anni.[92]

*

By the end of May the British government knows that the German and Soviet governments are secretly beginning to negotiate an agreement with the aim of dividing Eastern Europe between them. Sweden, Norway and Finland have refused Germany's offer of non-aggression pacts. On 15 May 1939 a woman's concentration camp opens at Ravensbruck, fifty miles north of Berlin and, on 22 May 1939, Germany and Italy sign the Pact of Steel.[93]

---

[92] Letter dated 28 May 1939 from Hulda Frankenbusch to Ilse Frankenbusch.

[93] Wikipedia. Op.cit. footnote 70.

# Chapter 4

## 1939
### June
### to
### August

At the beginning of June 1939 Hulda has been visiting Robert in Lagny. She tells Ilse that it was a very pleasant Sunday afternoon and they walked for over two hours along the River Marne. There was one swimming pool after another all very simple but free. The local government opens them for the summer tourists and the life guard gets 1 franc for looking after peoples belongings in the cabins. Hulda says that for 1 franc you can stay there all day. 'Idyllic', she says.

The rest of the letter is about Ilse and Roman's travel plans and about the parcel Ilse has received. Roman has sent Ilse a Dirndl which cost over 60 Marks. Hulda is a bit scathing. When will you wear something like that?" she asks, "Only at a fancy dress ball of Austrian refugees in New York or Rio".

*Heather, Ilse's granddaughter, wearing the dirndl in 2010*

She tells Ilse about a nude revue she went to at the "Alcazar" in the Rue Mazarine. It was called '*Caprice des Femmes*' and was "quite something', she says, 'those figures and bodies – splendid"[94]

*

A week later, Hulda is trying to encourage Ilse not to lose heart. Ilse has obviously been complaining about her work 'as a cook in a foreign household' because Hulda says that Ilse's circumstances are only the same as hundreds, probably thousands of girls have to put up with nowadays. Hulda reminds her that she has 'pure Jewish blood in your veins' and she has to prove that she will never give up.

Hulda says that her circumstances in Paris are exactly the same as Ilse's.

"I wake up in the morning and basically do not really know why I should get up, only to eat in a cafe, sit with any emigrant family and go back to sleep".

*Montmartre cafe scene 1939*

---

[94]   Letter dated 5 June 1939 from Hulda Frankenbusch to Ilse Frankenbusch.

"I lie in bed' she says, 'and go crazy about *Grossmuttl* [Grandmother], about you, about Anni and about this completely twisted world, of which one does not know whether it will blow up in chaos tomorrow!"

She tells Ilse that the problems with Roman will sort themselves out and says that it was always like that with them. They've always had crises and turn-arounds in their lives and just as they thought they could not go on, everything righted itself. They just have to hang in there and do something smarter than whine to each other.

Gisela has written that she may not be able to take anything with her when she leaves which would be a real pity, particularly for the nearly irreplaceable bed and table linen that Gisela still has.

"Still," she says, "gone is gone and there's no use crying over spilt milk."[95]

*

Eight days later an event took place in London that illustrates the preparations for war happening in Britain. About 7,500 people took part in the biggest Air Raid Precautions exercise the country had ever seen. Children and adults marched to 125 virtual shelters in the Chelsea area – i.e. chalked off areas to stand in and designated pubs. 400 wardens shepherded the crowds through the streets and 5000 children, many carrying blankets and gas masks, were taken to underground stations and then taken away again. Sirens were sounded for extra realism. As the streets were cleared, the Times reported that 'an unnatural silence fell', broken only by a loudspeaker announcement that the bombers were only seven or eight minutes away. A rocket was launched to give participants some idea of the noise of bombs falling. All traffic was stopped and had to park by the kerb and buses were emptied of passengers who were directed to the nearest shelter. Bomb damage was created for the purposes of the exercise and casualties were escorted to the first aid post at Chelsea Library.[96]

---

[95]    Letter dated 11 June 1939 from Hulda Frankenbusch to Ilse Frankenbusch.
[96]    The Library Time Machine. Ready for war – June 1939.
http://rbkclocalstudies.files.wordpress.com/2012/02/arp-exercise-1939-011.jpg .
Accessed 14.03 2013.

The people of London were preparing for a war that would be fought on their own doorsteps as well as in Europe but whether they were aware of what was coming is debatable. Certainly the bureaucrats and organisers of the exercise were and they tried to make it as realistic as was possible at the time.

*

The same day as the exercise in London, Gisela wrote to Ilse from Vienna in reply to a letter she has received from her granddaughter. Gisela writes that it is quite uncomfortable in the apartment now as the place is practically empty. Everything from mum's room, the dining room couch, the boxes from the kitchen, the sewing table and many smaller items are already gone. She is sleeping on a single bed and the hall armchairs are the only seats left. They've just had eight days of very cold weather which, she says, suits her 'because one cannot go anywhere anyway.' She ends by asking Ilse to write in English because it would be a very good exercise for them both and sends 'a million kisses'.[97]

*

In her next letter, Hulda reports on a meeting she has had with the Princess. She had written to her and was invited for afternoon tea at the *"Club Interalliee"* which was in a palace on the *Faubourg St. Honore* with a beautiful park in which they took tea. Then they went for 'a splendid car trip' and Hulda told Margarete all about the problems she was having. As a result she is going to meet with the Princess's lawyers who will take everything in hand – Gisela's immigration, luggage transportation, customs declarations etc. She also mentioned Ilse and Roman's possible emigration to the US and the Princess said she should bring that up with the lawyers as well. Margarete also said that she would reimburse Gisela's removal costs once she has arrived. Hulda was so happy about all this that she has already written to Gisela to try and give her some hope.

Ilse has obviously been complaining about her friend Hansi who she thinks is not working hard enough and Hulda comments that she never had a very high opinion of Hansi's competence and reliability. She says that Hansi has all the character traits that have given Jewish

---

[97]   Letter dated 19 June 1939 from Gisela Kerber to Ilse Frankenbusch.

82

girls a poor reputation and sometimes made it impossible for them to find work.

"You are yourself no ideal of patience," she tells Ilse, "but at least you have learned to work and that is something."[98]

*

Five days later Ilse receives a letter from Gisela who is very concerned about her granddaughter and worried that Hansi will pressure her into leaving a perfectly adequate job and good working conditions.

"Who knows what would await you both elsewhere," she writes.

Gisela tells her that her Aunt Olga Ammergut has died and asks that Ilse sends condolences to Aunt Julie Schafer, Olga's sister, at 9 *Hahngasse*, Wien 9. Gisela will go to her funeral because she is the only living close relative.

She tells Ilse what she will take with her to Paris – books, photos, pillows, duvets, crockery and cutlery. All this will stay in storage until Ilse can take possession of it.

"It is not a small matter to dissolve a household", she comments, "most items one must give away for free. So, for example, the books were given to the hospital and so many items I had to give away because no-one wanted to buy them."

However she is very excited about the news that the Princess is going to help with her visa which is taking so long to sort out.[99]

*

In Hulda's next letter she tells Ilse that she has given her a 'massive fright' because Ilse has written that she wants to go back to the Reich.

"Do you know what will be waiting for you?" she asks, "particularly with an Aryan passport?"

She tells Ilse that she will be forced into hard labour and doesn't think that serving a Nazi family as a farm labourer would appeal to her. She warns Ilse that she would not be allowed back into England with her German passport once she has left. Her English work permit

---

[98]  Letter dated 19 June 1939 from Hulda Frankenbusch to Ilse Frankenbusch.
[99]  Letter dated 24 June 1939 from Gisela Kerber to Ilse Frankenbusch.

will be cancelled automatically as soon as she leaves, her passport is only valid for one year and once it has expired she will be trapped. Apart from all that Hulda thinks it stupid to bring Roman into such danger which their meeting in the Reich will bring with it.

She begs Ilse "think things through before you do something. We just do not live in normal times so everything must be thought through."

She says that having a German passport will not be very helpful if she wants to go to the US. As in England, all the Czechs in Paris were requested to hand in their passports in exchange for German ones but most of them chose not to. Ilse had done as the German Embassy had requested which is why she now has a German passport.

Hulda writes "I prefer to be stateless than classed as a German citizen and," she says, "nothing would tempt me to go back to Vienna."

Hulda is annoyed with Ilse when she thinks that she moved 'heaven and earth' to get her out of Vienna and now she wants to go 'back under the knout' and all because of Roman.

"Hopefully," Hulda writes, "he is at least smart enough to advise you against it because he will know now that times have changed and to what danger you will expose yourself and also him."

She tells Ilse that she has heard from the Herzels in Fiume. Elly Herzel has died in a sanatorium in Gardone on Lake Garda of double pneumonia and her mother has been ill since Christmas with angiospasms – she has barely been out in the last six months and can only take a few steps round her room. 'Poor Uncle Frank', she says. She asks Ilse to write a few lines of condolence to Aunt Adele at *Via Pascoli* 4, Fiume. There does not seem to be much good news these days.

"*Grossmuttl*," she tells Ilse, "nags on my soul."

It is very unpleasant in Vienna nowadays and due to her migration Gisela has to deal with many authorities. In her last letter Gisela sounded quite down and upset which very much concerned Hulda.[100]

*

---

[100] Letter dated 25 June 1939 from Hulda Frankenbusch to Ilse Frankenbusch.

At the end of June 1939 the Womens Auxiliary Air Force was created in Britain, absorbing forty-eight RAF companies of the Auxiliary Territorial Service which have come into being since 1938. This was followed three days later by the Women's Land Army being re-formed to enable women to take over work in agriculture formerly done by young men who have now been drafted into the forces.[101] The countdown to war continues and the lives of the three women in Vienna, Paris and Aberdeen continue to be affected by world events while at the same time they remain most concerned about the minutiae of their daily lives and those of their extended family.

*

By July, Ilse has given up on the idea of going to Germany and Hulda warns her to make sure she's not forced to go. If she hadn't exchanged her Czech passport for a German one she'd now be stateless and the UK couldn't expel her, but with a German passport she could be expelled if war was declared. Hulda says again 'patience, patience and more patience!' and tells Ilse that a year of separation from Roman is not that long – especially in the present circumstances.

She writes that Ilse's father, Rudolf, had to get out of Holland 'at breakneck speed' and this shows that the Dutch fear all kinds of 'complications' and want as few foreigners as possible in the country. She wonders whether '*Vatl*' [Father] was already in England and whether he's started his job yet.

On a lighter note, she tells Ilse about a trip to Versailles to a night festival with Dr and Frau Kris. They had been given four tickets and were seated in the stalls on the stage where a seat normally costs 50 francs.

"It was as lovely as a fairytale," writes Hulda.

The whole performance took place in the lower part of the garden. In the middle of the lake was a huge floating stage on which the Paris Opera Ballet danced both traditional and modern dances with a lot of costume changes and lighting effects. Then all the fountains sprang

---

[101]   Wikipedia. 1939 in the United Kingdom.
http://en.wikipedia.org/wiki/1939_in_the_United_Kingdom. Accessed 3 March 2013.

into life, all lit up in different ways and after that was a huge firework display.

"Then," she says, "the moon shone and it was like a dream."

She said to Frau Kris time and again 'Why isn't Ilse here?! She would love it.' Hulda becomes melancholy again and laments the fate of parents 'I need you so much but I will have to do without you for the rest of my life'. On a more positive note, she is meeting with the princess and her lawyers in two days time and hopes for some resolution to 'Grandmother's affair'.[102]

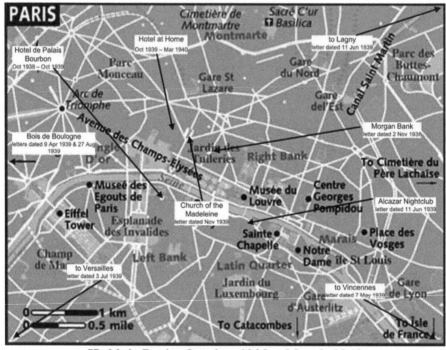

*Hulda's Paris, October 1938 – March 1940*

\*

The next letter from Hulda is typewritten. She tells Ilse that it is Sani's machine but Hulda is looking after it for him and will use it while she can. Ilse has handed in her resignation in Aberdeen and has four more weeks to work before she can leave. She plans to take two weeks off and have a holiday in Bournemouth before she starts work again. Hulda has had letters from Gisela and Anni and Gisela has

---

[102] Letter dated 3 July 1939 from Hulda Frankenbusch to Ilse Frankenbusch.

86

mentioned a matter that Hulda considers too dangerous to write about – especially just before her leaving. She decides on a code they could use to discuss this matter in their letters. Anni has offered to keep Ilse's things at their place in Holland for which Hulda is very grateful because it would cost a lot in storage if it was sent to Paris as Gisela suggested. Anni wants Hulda to visit her in the autumn but she doesn't know if she should leave Gisela so soon on her own in Paris. Hulda has now finished with the dentist.

"My mouth looks wonderful," she says, "but in total it cost nearly 1500 francs – quite a chunk of money."

There has also been a letter from Szerina in London and Hulda cannot understand why Alice, who has married so well, allows her mother to work so hard.[103]

*

A letter from Hulda in mid July tells Ilse that friends have told her that if Ilse can cook well she will not have a problem finding a position immediately she arrives in England. Ilse is planning to travel from Aberdeen to London by boat and Hulda envies her the trip but warns her about spending all her money so she doesn't suddenly find herself penniless. That is Hulda's own worst nightmare.

Ilse is now planning to go to Holland to meet up with Roman and once again Hulda warns her to make sure she can get back into England again with her German passport. Hulda thinks that anyone entering Holland on a German passport will immediately be deported over the border into the Reich. She encloses Anni's last letter which illustrates what is happening in Holland at the moment.

Hulda mentions that Robert is still in Lagny and doing well on his agricultural course.

"He is getting fat," she says, "and looks like a farmer."

He isn't very happy with Hulda at the moment because she isn't giving him any more money. As always, Hulda is worried about money and what with dentist bills, Gisela about to arrive and having to find somewhere new for them to live together, she says 'it is one big headache'. She will get reimbursed for her living expenses by the

---

[103]   Letter dated 9 July 1939 from Hulda Frankenbusch to ilse Frankenbusch.

Princess but not until the end of August when Margarete gets back from her spa holiday in Vichy and that seems a long way away.

Meanwhile, Paris is celebrating 150 years of revolution.

"My head is buzzing with all the Tra-ra and Boom-boom," says Hulda, "but really it is very nice!"

She is enclosing the official programme with her letter and has marked the parts she has been to. One day she didn't get home until 2.30am – she was on her feet from 9am until lunchtime when she had a siesta and then in the evening until midnight after which she sat in the *Cafe de la Paix* and watched the people in the street until 2am when she walked home. There was dancing in all the squares and, she says 'it was quite something.' There were lots of soldiers around in their different uniforms which made the Parisian street scene particularly gay and lively. Lots of different regiments were represented including English marines and English guards – she tells Ilse that 'your tall lads in their red jackets have really enjoyed themselves!' She tells Ilse about two soldiers from the French Foreign Legion who came into the Viennese *Café Luzian* in their well-known uniforms and when the waiter gave them a menu and asked them in French what they would like, one of them replied in a broad East Hungarian dialect 'Be so good as to make me a huge veal cutlet – I haven't eaten anything like that in ages.' The other one, not to be outdone, added in pure Budapest German, equally unmistakable, 'I would like a genuine Hungarian Goulash.' The rest of the guests broke into applause and they got their cutlet and goulash free of charge plus as much cheese, fruit, desert, beer and wine as they wanted.

Hulda comments "They could have been criminals and the lowest of the low for who knows who is in the Foreign Legion nowadays?!"

Hulda talks about Sani who sends his best wishes to Ilse. She doesn't see much of him nowadays – not since he moved out of the hotel – sometimes only once a week. He has so many friends and is invited out such a lot, especially since he got his journalist ID card.

"Between you and me," Hulda says, "I'm sure he could get me a ticket to go somewhere sometimes and could take me with him, but I believe I am not elegant or suitable enough for him and probably also not young enough!"

She tells Ilse that if she were in Paris he would probably be happy enough to take her out. As Ilse knows, Sani himself is well endowed and likes to go out with women who somehow make a striking impression. 'I can't be any use to him in this respect!' acknowledges Hulda[104]

*

Gisela writes two letters very similar in content to Ilse over the next week. Gisela is very worried about her granddaughter giving up her position in Aberdeen and is wondering what she will do next, will she get paid more and whether Hansi is still with her. Gisela's luggage is now at the freight forwarders and the Foreign Currency Control Centre has issued the authorisation for it to leave Vienna. All that's needed now is the custom's inspection and then it will be on its way. Ilse's belongings have already left and are on their way to Anni's in Rotterdam. The only luggage Gisela has now is one suitcase and that will be her hand luggage when she leaves. She asks about Ilse's father – whether Ilse has heard from him and whether he is London and working as a chemist.[105]

In the later letter Gisela tells Ilse not to worry about her being homeless. She says she can stay in the *Blechturmgasse* apartment until the 11 August and if she hasn't received her visa by then she will need to rent another room. She has been offered 'sleeping accommodation' at 1 *Esslingasse* with old Frau Lowig whose children are already in England. She mentions that 'Uncle Otto gets baptised tomorrow'.[106] Uncle Otto is in Prague and is probably hedging his bets and hoping he can pass as a Christian.

*

At the end of July the Princess receives a letter from her lawyers advising her that they have received notification from the *Ministere des Affaires Etrangeres* saying that the application for a 'passport visa for Madame Gisele Kerber is receiving the consideration of the Ministry of the Interior and that as soon as advise is received ... Foreign Affairs will take a decision which they will communicate immediately to the *Consulat General de France'* in Vienna.

[104]  Letter dated 16 July 1939 from Hulda Frankenbusch to ilse Frankenbusch.
[105]  Letter dated 19 July 1939 from Gisela Kerber to Ilse Frankenbusch.
[106]  Letter dated 24 July 1939 from Gisela Kerber to Ilse Frankenbusch.

Unfortunately, nothing new has happened since the matter was handed over to the Princess's lawyers – Hulda and Gisela are in exactly the same position as they were before.[107]

*

Another short letter from Gisela indicates that she has received a letter from Ilse saying that she and Hansi will not be working together in future and also telling Gisela that her father has a good position and may be able to help Ilse get a job with the same company. Gisela also tells Ilse that Aunt Irma and Hans (Ilse's cousin) are in London and that the whole family have got an entry visa to Brazil but that they are going to try and make a go of it in London first. She tells Ilse that she will forward on their address once she has it 'as one never knows when one might need it'.[108]

*

The beginning of August sees Hulda getting more and more desperate as still, nothing seems to be happening with Gisela's visa. She has heard from Gisela that the customs inspection for the luggage has gone smoothly and that it will be on its way out of Austria very soon. Meanwhile Ilse's belongings are on their way to Anni and so, Hulda says, they 'are rescued'. She is worried because she hasn't heard from Ilse and isn't sure whether she is still in Aberdeen or has already left. There's not much news from Paris, she says, - the weather is better, she has had a cold and is getting headaches and Sani is at present in Amsterdam and will ring Anni in Rotterdam. Before he left he got Hulda a ticket for the *Folies Bergeres* which she didn't find very exciting, 'still the same old chorus line' she tells Ilse.[109]

*

A few days later Ilse hears from her grandmother. Gisela is writing in the kitchen because she doesn't have a table or chair in her room any more. It looks terrible but she has managed to get rid of everything for which she is glad. The breaking up of the household has been hard and has hurt her terribly but, she says, 'it will soon be over now'. She

---

[107] Letter dated 25 July 1939 from Coudert Brothers Paris to Princess Boncompagni.
[108] Letter dated 26 July 1939 from Gisela Kerber to Ilse Frankenbusch.
[109] Letter dated 1 August 1939 from Hulda Frankenbusch to Ilse Frankenbusch.

has sent Ilse a bra she has asked for and if it fits will send another – the same with the stockings. She tells Ilse that Aunt Schafer has had four people allocated to her apartment. 'What a life' she comments. She signs herself 'your already really old *Grossmuttl*'.[110]

*

The Nazis believed that all Jewish property belonged to the Reich and by August 1939 had seized more than half of the Jewish apartments in Vienna. As many as five or six families were forced to live in one apartment and the resulting sanitary problems became 'evidence' that Jews needed to be deported. The Nazis had tried to force the remaining Jews in Vienna to move into a single area of the city, Wien 2, in order to make it easier for them to control their movements. Many of those remaining were old and sick and unable to endure the process of obtaining the necessary paperwork needed to emigrate, let alone move to a new country.[111]

*

From Hulda's next letter we learn that Ilse has left Aberdeen and is enjoying her holiday in Bournemouth. Ilse must have complained about the amount of work she had to do in her last four weeks because Hulda comments that she is 'not surprised because of the attitude of the Scots'.

"However," she says, "at least you proved until the end that immigrants are worth employing".

She tells Ilse that Sani has returned from Holland with her typewriter from Anni and a food parcel of cakes, tea and marmalade. Anni and Wim brought the parcels to the railway station and Sani told Hulda that Anni looked very well and he liked Wim very much.

"Apart from that," Hulda says, "he is as unenthusiastic about Holland as we are."

She tells Ilse that Sani is going to Budapest for a few weeks and will stop off in Vienna to talk to Gisela. She has already written to her mother to let her know about her upcoming visitor.

"He really is a good fellow!" she says.

---

[110] Letter 4 August 1939 from Gisela Kerber to Ilse Frankenbusch.
[111] Mills, Jan-Ruth. The Holocaust in Austria. Unpublished and undated article.

Gisela has written to Hulda to tell her that she is moving to *Esslingasse* 13 in Wien 1 and Hulda thinks she will be more comfortable there. *Esslingasse* is a nice quiet street of typical Viennese apartment buildings. There are tree lined streets at either end and a pleasant square, the *Borse Platz*, is not far away. The entrance to the street is on the main road alongside the canal and so is a convenient place to live.[112]

"Grandma will only have one room to worry about and keep clean" says Hulda "and she will be with people who know her, want her to be there and will be good to her".

She is only paying 25 RM a month which is not much.

Hulda talks about the newspaper cuttings and magazine articles she will now start sending to Birmingham, including one about conditions in Brazil and another about Vienna. She reminds Ilse that Bournemouth is near the place where Herta Miskoloczy is working and says that the next time she sees Robert she will get the address. She also tells Ilse that Walter and Irma Lange are now in London as is Poldi Squarenina with his second wife.

She's worried about Ilse being in either London or Birmingham because of the Irish bombs and says Bournemouth would be a lot safer because it's not an industrial centre. She ends by sending her greetings to 'Father" and a thousand kisses to Ilse.[113]

*

On the same day, Gisela has also written a short letter to Ilse. She tells Ilse that she has got her new address from her father but not to expect a long letter because she is tired from the move and, being alone, she has a hundred things that need doing. It's been a hot day and she's been sweating profusely. She tells Ilse that Roman, who helped her move, looks fine but is desperate to leave and asks whether Rudolf, Ilse's father, could help somehow. She asks Ilse to write soon and says she can only keep going because of Ilse's and Hulda's letters.[114]

---

[112] Email dated 28 August 2009 from Helen Powles to Sonia Waterfall.
[113] Letter dated 8 August 1939 from Hulda Frankenbusch to Ilse Frankenbusch.
[114] Letter dated 8 August 1939 from Gisela Kerber to Ilse Frankenbusch.

My beloved Goldengirl!

Yesterday I received your little card and luckily I got the address from Vatl.
So I will write to you immediately.
Only you cannot expect a long letter because I am tired from the move and I am all alone and one has to do 100 things. And the heat! Beads of sweat are running from my forehead. You have already my new address. Hopefully you got the new bra. Today I could send you 1 large envelope; parcels are difficult to send. Roman looks fine – but he would like to leave. Can't father help somehow!

Write soon; tell me "everything" and think of your Grandmother who lives nurtured only by your and your mothers letters.
Regard to father and to you kisses from your Großmuttl.

*Letter from Gisela to Ilse, August 1939*

\*

In mid August Hulda writes to the Princess's lawyers, quoting from a letter from Margarete where she says "I'm sure Mr Robinson will be glad to help you if you write him". Hulda asks Mr John Robinson if he can do anything to hurry the formalities at the Ministry of the Interior and the decision of Foreign Affairs, while at the same time giving him Gisela's new address.[115] She gets an answer almost immediately saying that they have written again to the Ministry of the Interior but reminding her that 'sometimes during the summer vacation, these matters are unusually slow'.[116]

\*

When Hulda next writes to her daughter, Ilse has arrived in Birmingham and plans to stay at least eight days with her father. Hulda says

---

[115] Letter dated 12 August 1939 from Hulda Frankenbusch to Mr John Robinson of Coudert Brothers, Paris.

[116] Letter dated 18 August 1939 from Coudert Brothers, Paris to Hulda Frankenbusch.

"I have heard that Birmingham is a dirty industrial city unlike Bournemouth which must be a very pleasant place according to the British travel agents here".

Hulda asks after Hansi, whether Ilse has any news from Rudi in Rio and comments that she is not surprised that Roman couldn't get a visa for Brazil. Hulda is at her wits end about what more she can do for Gisela.

"My nerves are already so shaken", she says, "that every time I receive a letter from *Grossmuttl*, my heart is racing and afterwards I am crying most of the night"

She tells Ilse that the spokesperson of the Princess got a letter from the ministry stating that 'everything will run its course'. The Princess has written from Vichy saying that Hulda should be patient until the beginning of September when Margarete will be back in Paris and will get in touch.

"These people don't take our situation seriously enough," comments Hulda, "they have ample time to do things and are surprised at our urgency. One cannot make them understand how much depends on it. All they can see is that one is alive, has a roof over our head and is not hungry. Of course they are right, there is so much misery in the world that we can all be grateful."

She tells Ilse to be careful with her money as who knows when she will have an income, and talks about her own money worries. The Princess has promised to reimburse her when she gets back to Paris but that is still a few weeks away.

"And you know how petrified I am about suddenly being without money," Hulda writes.

She ends her letter by saying "Don't be so unhappy! I am already unhappy enough for both of us!"[117]

*

International events were about to take over the lives of the three women once again. Throughout August both German-Soviet negotiations and Tripartite negotiations, between Britain, France and the Soviets, had been in progress. The Tripartite negotiations sought an

---

[117] Letter dated 14 August 1939 from Hulda Frankenbusch to Ilse Frankenbusch.

agreement on the reaction of the three powers to a German attack. The British feared communism and didn't trust Stalin. They didn't treat the negotiations with any sense of urgency and sent a minor official, who had to refer all decisions back to London, to Moscow to deal with Stalin. The Soviets wanted to move troops through Poland to attack Germany in the event of an alliance with Britain and France. Poland refused to allow Soviet troops into the country because they believed that once the Red Army entered their territory they wouldn't leave. This was a sticking point for the Tripartite negotiations and the talks dragged on. Meanwhile Stalin turned to the Germans.[118]

The German-Soviet Pact, also known as the Ribbentrop-Molotov Pact after the two foreign ministers who negotiated the agreement, was in two parts. The first was an economic agreement, signed on 19 August 1939 provided for the exchange of manufactured goods from Germany for raw materials from Russia.[119] On 21 August the Soviets suspended the Tripartite talks and let the Germans know that they would be amenable to signing a non-aggression pact. This was finally signed in the late hours of 23 August 1939.

In the Treaty of Non-Aggression between Germany and the Soviet Union, each signatory agreed not to attack the other. The treaty also included a secret protocol that divided the territories of Romania, Poland, Lithuania, Latvia, Estonia and Finland into Nazi and Soviet 'spheres of influence'.[120] The treaty provided Stalin with time to settle issues with Japan on his eastern border and time to make military preparations for the war against Germany that he knew was inevitable. It freed up Hitler to invade Poland without having to contend with a Soviet threat from the east. It ended British hopes of an alliance with Russia to stop Hitler and the British people realised that nothing would stop him now except war. It was instrumental in causing the Second World War.[121]

*

---

[118]   Clare, John. The Nazi-Soviet Pact of 1939.
       http://www.johndclare.net/RoadtoWWII8.htm . Accessed 20 April 2013.
[119]   United States Holocaust Memorial Museum. Holocaust Encyclopedia. German-Soviet Pact. http://www.ushmm.org/wlc/en/article.php?ModuleId=10005156. Accessed 20 April 2013.
[120]   Wikipedia. Molotov-Ribbentrop Pact. http://en.wikipedia.org/wiki/Molotov %E2%80%93Ribbentrop_Pact. Accessed 27 March 2013.
[121]   Clare, John. Op.cit. footnote 118.

Meanwhile Hulda continued writing to Ilse. In a letter written on the same day that the Soviets suspended the Tripartite talks, Hulda talks about Ilse's stay in Birmingham. She tells Ilse not to worry about hurting her because she's staying with her father. Hulda says that she is a bit sad but that will pass and she'd much rather Ilse be employed as an interpreter than as a cook. She encourages Ilse to read a lot in English and get some technical books about glassmaking from the factory and browse through them.

"You will realise," she says, "that there will be repeated phrases and if you familiarise yourself with them you are winning already."

Hulda is worried about Ilse's loneliness but says it's the same for her and that there are some days when the only person she speaks to is the waitress in the restaurant. However, she is enjoying the weather and has been swimming a few times, three days to the pool and once outside at Dr.Kris's place on the banks of the Seine. The latter resulted in a sunburnt back and she was unable to move or get dressed for two days and now her back is so itchy it's driving her crazy.

She asks Ilse to tell her all about Birmingham – about the city, where she lives, what her life is like, does she eat in a restaurant. She wonders what the factory is like and what it's like working in a mainly male environment.

"I want to know all," she says, "because as soon as it involves you I am very nosey – you know that."

Nothing much has changed in Paris, the solicitor is still working on Gisela's visa, she hasn't seen much of Robert lately and she has had a fight with Dr. Kris and isn't speaking to him at the moment.[122]

As details of the Molotov-Ribbentrop Pact become public on 24 August, Neville Chamberlain recalled Parliament several weeks early. In a burst of legislation a War Powers Act is passed, the Navy is put on a war footing, all forces leave is cancelled, the coastal defence reserves are called up and Civil Defence workers are placed on alert. On 25 August the German Foreign Ministry cuts off all telegraph and telephone communication with the outside world.[123]

---

[122] Letter dated 21 August 1939 from Hulda Frankenbusch to Ilse Frankenbusch.
[123] Wikipedia. Op.cit. footnote 101.

Hulda writes to Ilse that she took her letter to the coffee house in the *Bois de Boulogne*. She says that there is no peace at the hotel any longer and she was glad to escape. She is hoping that the postal service to England is still running as the borders to Germany seem to be closed.

"Poor *Grossmuttl*," she says, "She will have to have a lot of patience and faces uncomfortable times, as do we all."

"For me it's like the time of Hitler's march into Vienna," Hulda writes, "I am full of fear and afraid of what will happen to us. Can you remember how nervous and afraid I was that night," she asks Ilse, "well now it's the same – only then you crawled into bed with me and all was well again! And now I'm lying alone at night and am afraid!"

She now has an 'escape suitcase' next to the bed and in it she's put pyjama pants, two pairs of thick socks, towels, handkerchiefs, paper serviettes, a complete set of toiletries, bandages and medicines, candles and matches, a good torch, sugar cubes, smoked sausage etc. Her papers and money she carries in her handbag at all times. She has also bought herself a large suitcase and packed into it everything she had in cartons or drawers including all the linen and clothes that Gisela had sent.

"So if they evacuate all foreigners," she says, "I can deposit it into storage."

"However", she writes, "viewing Parisian life from the outside nothing has really changed. The garden cafe here is today as it was last week and the really very good quintet has just finished playing 'The Blue Danube'."

In the metro that day she had met a couple from Breslau. They arrived in Paris the day before and are continuing on to Chile in ten days time. He spent 18 months in Buchenwald and the fact that they could sit on a bench in the *Bois* and go where they pleased gave them so much pleasure.

"It was rather touching", comments Hulda.

Answering Ilse's letter, Hulda says that it is good that Ilse is with her father in these uncertain times and is not alone. There is now no chance of Ilse visiting Hulda in Paris or Hulda coming to London. She went to see Mr Wynn at Morgan Bank two days ago and asked him if she should voluntarily leave for the provinces but he advised her not to and said she should wait in Paris and see what happens. He reassured her that she would always get her allowance from the Princess and said that the bank didn't close for a single day during the last war and he couldn't see why anything should be different this time.

To finish the letter she comments on Ilse's description of her experiences with her father which, she says, amused her greatly.

"Well," she says, "he really has not learned much, and it's questionable whether you can change him. I wish you the best of luck! You'll have to have a lot of patience. One thing you can tell *Vatl* from me: he should not delude himself that he will be accepted on equal terms in British society. Even if he were a company director and earned millions he will always be a 'foreigner', he might be honoured and accepted for his expertise in the workplace, but never fully accepted in society. And especially not if he does not manage to absorb, totally absorb, the English habits and customs. In this the English are rather intolerant. Well, do you think that Vatl will do that?! With his self importance and his idea that he knows everything better than anyone else?!"

A note in the margin tells Ilse that she doesn't have a gas mask as there are none to be had, whereas in London everybody got one – even the immigrants. She ends with the hope that the mail system will keep functioning as she is continually waiting for the next mail delivery.[124]

*

A day later and Warsaw is preparing itself for war. Trenches are being dug, power stations sandbagged and people have started carrying gas masks around with them. Danzig remains the flashpoint of the Polish-Nazi conflict as Hitler believes that Danzig should be returned to Germany and that the Polish corridor should be cut in half by linking East Prussia and the rest of Germany with a band of territory.

In England the government published a list of 104 emergency regulations for the defence of Great Britain. They are split up into several sections.

The first deals with the security of the state and prevents people from spying or interfering with essential services. It also covers

---

[124] Letter dated 27 August 1939 from Hulda Frankenbusch to Ilse Frankenbusch.

impersonating police officers, interfering with radio communications, carrying a camera in certain designated areas and the stricter control of homing pigeons.

The second section deals with public safety and will affect everyone by providing for the compulsory evacuation of people, animals and moveable property on the orders of the Secretary of State. It also deals with the precautions to be taken in the event of an air attack, such as the use of shelters, the co-ordination of fire brigades and police forces and the control of lighting during darkness.

The third section gives the Admiralty control over merchant shipping and aircraft.

The regulations also contain wide-ranging powers for the requisitioning of land and property, the control of industry as well as the control of road and rail traffic.

On the same day as the emergency regulations were published a full-scale rehearsal of evacuation plans took place. 900 schools in London and other cities took part involving over a million children.[125]

*

Hulda's last letter to Ilse before the outbreak of war was also written on the same day. Hulda had heard from Gisela and comments that at least she is healthy but doesn't seem to have any idea of what is going on. It's the same with some people in Paris and the couple from Breslau that she met two days ago had no idea that the city was preparing for war. The good news from Gisela is that Anni has already received Ilse's belongings so at least they're now out of Germany.[126]

*

By the final days of August most paintings had been evacuated from the National Gallery in London to an unknown destination in Wales, the evacuation of children from major UK cities had begun and Poland had begun mobilising its troops against Nazi Germany.[127] In Vienna, a new round of measures had been taken against the Jews. On

---

[125]  BBC. Countdown to World War II.
http://www.bbc.co.uk/history/worldwars/wwtwo/countdown_390828_mon_01.sh
tml. Accessed 20 April 2013.
[126]  Letter dated 28 August 1939 from Hulda Frankenbusch to Ilse Frankenbusch.
[127]  Wikipedia. Op.cit. footnote 101.

the eve of war, the Nazis requisitioned all precious metals, leaving Jews with only their wedding rings, watches and a table serving for two.[128]

[128] Encyclopaedia Judaica. Jews in Austria 1938-1945. http://www.geschichteinchronologbie.ch/eu/oe/encJud_juden-in-oe05-1938-1945-ENG... Accessed 20 April 2013.

# Chapter 5

## 1939

### September
### to
### December

At 4.45am on 1 September 1939, the battleship *Schleswig-Holstein* commenced firing on the fortress *Westerplatte*, a Polish army installation at the mouth of the port of Danzig in Poland. Simultaneously German *Wehrmacht* troops began crossing the border into Poland. World War II had begun.

*Invasion of Poland, September 1938*

In Britain the blackout was imposed across the country, the BBC Home Service began broadcasting and the army was officially mobilised. Norway, Finland, Sweden and Switzerland declare their neutrality. The following day Danzig was annexed to Nazi Germany and Spain and Ireland declared their neutrality.[129]

On September 3, Neville Chamberlain told the House of Commons that England was officially at war with Germany, together with France, Australia and New Zealand. Shortly after 11am Chamberlain announced the news on BBC Radio from 10 Downing Street. Christopher Isherwood, listening with a friend, described his feelings.

"It was as if neither of us were present. The living room seemed absolutely empty – with nothing in it but the announcer's voice. No fear, no despair, no sensation at all. Just hollowness."[130]

---

[129] Wikipedia. http://en.wikipedia.org/wiki/1939. Accessed 3 March 2013.

Twenty minutes later air raid sirens sounded in London – it was a false alarm. Chamberlain created a small war Cabinet which included Winston Churchill as First Lord of the Admiralty. In the Admiralty office that evening, Churchill found his old charts of the North Sea with which he had planned battles and blockades in the last war and a signal went out to the British fleet: WINSTON IS BACK.[131]

Life magazine said 'The second Armageddon is on'.[132]

*

In Hulda's first letter of September she sounds very subdued.

"We cannot lose our nerve now," she tells Ilse, "we can only hope that we get out of this mess as we have done so many times in our lives."

The worst thing that has happened so far to Hulda is that the hotel has painted all the windows dark blue – a cheaper option to blackout paper. She says 'the house and rooms are smelling awfully of this oil paint'. She also tells Ilse that Mr Recht was taken to the Prefecture the night before to provide some information, so they said, but he hasn't come back. So maybe he has been imprisoned. Hulda has spent all day with Mrs Recht to comfort her but she is a bit wary about being seen too much in their company because who knows what he did to be taken away.

"However", she says, "the fact that this could happen is, in itself, very depressing!"

She has been told that the hotel might have to close in a couple of weeks' time and doesn't know what she will do. Also she hasn't heard from Gisela for over a week and doesn't know if the mail is getting through so she is going to try writing to Vienna via Holland and see if that works.[133]

*

[130] Baker, Nicholson. Human smoke: the beginnings of World War II, the end of civilisation. London, Simon & Schuster, 2008. p. 136.
[131] Wikipedia. 1939 in the United Kingdom.
http://en.wikipedia.org/wiki/1939_in_the_United_kingdom. Accessed 3 March 2013.
[132] Baker Nicholson. Op.cit. footnote 130, p.138.
[133] Letter dated 3 September 1939 from Hulda Frankenbusch to Ilse Frankenbusch.

In the coming days Canada and South Africa declare war on Germany and the United States declares its neutrality. In Britain, the National Services (Armed Forces) Act is passed introducing conscription for all men aged 18 to 41. On 3 September 1939 the British liner SS Athenia becomes the first civilian casualty of the war when she is sunk by the German submarine U-30 with the loss of 117 lives. A day later the first raid by the Royal Air Force on German shipping takes place and on 9 September the British Expeditionary Force crosses to France.

*

Hulda writes postcards for the rest of the month, the first being to tell Ilse that the hotel is closing and she is moving on 9 September to 'the little hotel on the *Rue de Surene*' where Roman stayed when he was there over Christmas. They have had 'three alerts', presumably air raid warnings, but Hulda said they all went well except during the last one she had a 'severe heart attack'. She now has medicine for her heart which she hopes will do her good. Her new address is 'Hotel at Home, 27 *Rue de Surene*, Paris 8' and she asks Ilse to send it to Anni whom she hasn't heard from in some time. The postcard is addressed to Ilse at c/o Grey Friars, 1 Portland Road, Edgbaston, Birmingham[134]

From the next postcard it seems that there are almost nightly 'alerts' and Hulda says it's eight days since she got a good nights' sleep.

"But," she says, "we will no doubt get used to this sort of life."

She is worried about Gisela and says "What shall become of your grandma? Shall I ever see my mother again? Can you imagine my anxiety? Also about you and Anni!"[135]

In the next postcard Hulda bewails the fact that she hasn't heard from Ilse. Anni has written and let Hulda know that she has had news from her sister and that Ilse is well. Anni has also forwarded a letter and a card from Gisela who seems to be alright. Hulda is very glad to have news of her. She is spending her time mainly at the hotel in her room, trying to stay calm.

---

[134] Postcard dated 7 September 1939 from Hulda Frankenbusch to Ilse Frankenbusch.
[135] Postcard dated 11 September 1939 from Hulda Frankenbusch to Ilse Frankenbusch.

"I do not know," she says, "if they will allow us to stay in Paris. If only I knew where to go!"

She asks whether Ilse will stay in Birmingham and whether she has heard from Hansi and Roman. She ends with kindest regards to 'your father' which is how she refers to her ex-husband, Rudolf.[136]

By the end of the month Hulda has heard from Ilse that she is well and busy furnishing Rudolf's flat in Birmingham. Hulda is wondering whether to go and stay with Anni in Rotterdam.

"But," she says, "I do not think that Holland is any safer than France. For the moment we are alright here in Paris but naturally nobody knows what will come next."

She is worried about money again and tells Ilse she has to pay for the storage of the luggage Gisela has sent from Vienna as well as send some money to her next month. Ilse seems to be worried about her mother's health because Hulda tells her not to worry – some days she feels nervy and sick, other days she's alright.

"I will try and be as strong as possible," she writes, "because I want to live to see you, my dear girl, happy and lucky."[137]

\*

By 15 September 1939 German troops had surrounded Warsaw and the siege of the city had begun. The following day the Soviets signed a ceasefire with Japan in the east, thus freeing them up to move into Poland which they did on 17 September, occupying eastern Polish territories. By 19 September the siege of Warsaw was over and German troops were on the verge of taking over the city. 22 September saw a joint victory parade of *Wehrmacht* and Red Army troops marking the end of the invasion of Poland and by the end of the month Nazi Germany and the Soviet Union had agreed on a division of Poland. Already, Heydrich, chief of the Security Police, had issued a directive for all Jews living in towns and villages in the occupied zones of Poland to be transferred to ghettos and for Jewish Councils,

---

[136] Postcard dated 17 September 1939 from Hulda Frankenbusch to Ilse Frankenbusch.
[137] Postcard dated 25 September 1939 from Hulda Frankenbusch to Ilse Frankenbusch.

*Judenrate*, to be established to carry out the orders of the German authorities.[138]

In England fascist politician William Joyce had already begun broadcasting Nazi propaganda under the name Lord Haw-Haw. Petrol rationing had begun and identity cards introduced.[139]

In Vienna, all Jews lived under martial law and additional restrictions were imposed upon them. Jews could no longer attend sporting events, were banned completely from parks and public gardens and Jewish lawyers and doctors could no longer have non-Jewish clients. By the end of September they were not allowed to go out after 8pm or listen to the radio, measures which made mass arrests easier. With the outbreak of war emigration possibilities lessened considerably and 17,000 Jews possessing entry visas to enemy countries were forbidden to use them.[140]

*

In Hulda's first postcard of October she tells Ilse that on the same day that her letter arrived she also got one from Anni and Gisela.

"The latter," she says, "seems to be alright, just nervous and depressed at having to stay alone in Vienna not knowing what will happen next."

Gisela seems anxious about money but Hulda doesn't know what she can do about it and has asked Anni to investigate whether she can do anything through her bank.

"Here in Paris," she writes, "everything is quiet. We had an 'alert' on Friday morning but nothing really in earnest. As long as I get 4-5 hours of sleep at night my health seems to get better."[141]

The next communication from Hulda is a letter and she has had a long letter from Ilse and two from Gisela. One came through Mr Kun in Budapest and one through Anni in Rotterdam. Gisela writes that Roman is very unhappy, not having had any news from Ilse and he

---

138  Wikipedia. Op.cit. footnote 129.
139  Wikipedia. Op.cit. footnote 131.
140  Encyclopaedia Judaica. Jews in Austria 1938-1945. http://www.geschichteinchronologie.ch/eu/oe/EncJud_juden-in-oe05-1938-1945-ENG...Accessed 20 April 2013.
141  Postcard dated 2 October 1939 from Hulda Frankenbusch to Ilse Frankenbusch.

fears that she doesn't love him or want him anymore and is trying to push him away. Gisela has tried to reassure him and make it clear that he has to be patient. Hulda says that there is nothing else to do but be patient and wait these times out. They would all like to be together but it's impossible to do anything about it at the moment.

She tells Ilse not to worry about her – she can take care of herself, is eating enough and if it wasn't for her 'heart-jumping' episodes she would be alright. As long as she takes her medicine, she can keep these episodes at bay.

"The main person to worry about," she says, "is Grandma and the thought that I might not see my mother again is such a bad feeling. I wonder whether she has enough to eat, will she get through the winter without getting sick, will she get the money I send her and, if not, will there be anyone to help her through? All these thoughts go round and round in my poor head."

She begs Ilse to write more long letters and says "That is the only pleasure I have now."[142]

*

A letter to Ilse from the Aliens Registration Office of Birmingham City Police is worth quoting in full. It is addressed to Ilse Frankenbusch of 1 Portland Road, Edgbaston, Birmingham and says:

"Tribunals have been appointed by the Secretary of State to examine the position of all Germans and Austrians over the age of 16 in this country, and to consider which of them can properly be exempted from interment and which of those exempted from interment can be exempted also from the special restrictions which are imposed by the Aliens Order on enemy aliens, i.e, the restrictions on travelling without a travel permit, on change of residence without the permission of the police, and on the possession without a police permit of certain articles including motor cars, cameras, etc .

---

[142] Letter dated 14 October 1939 from Hulda Frankenbusch to Ilse Frankenbusch.

**Letter to Ilse re the Aliens Tribunal, October 1939**

Your case will be considered by the tribunal sitting at Victoria Law Courts, Corporation Street, Birmingham, and you should attend there on October 21 1939 at 2pm. You should bring with you your Police Registration Certificate.

If you are well-known to a British subject or to someone who has lived here for a long time or are in the employment of such a person, you should ask such a person to state in writing what he or she knows about you, and you should bring the statement with you. You can also invite such a person to attend in case the tribunal wants to put any questions to him or her.

Legal representatives (solicitors or barristers) will not be allowed to act as advocate before the tribunal.

If you are unable to attend in accordance with this notice, you should send me without delay a statement in writing explaining the reason."

It was signed by J.D.Wild, Secretary, Aliens Tribunal, Birmingham Area.[143]

This must have been a frightening experience for Ilse, especially as she still had her German passport at this time. However, she must only

---

[143] Letter dated 19 October 1939 from J.D.Wild of the Aliens Tribunal, Birminbham to Ilse Frankenbusch.

have mentioned it in passing to Hulda who, in a later letter, merely asks Ilse to explain what an Aliens Tribunal is.

*

In Hulda's next letter she is worried because Ilse has fallen out with her father and is very unhappy.

"I knew beforehand" Hulda says, "that it would turn out like this, but my hope was that the exceptional times that we are experiencing would make both you and your father a bit more patient."

Ilse must have suggested that she should join her mother in Paris but Hulda says that there is nothing she can do to help Ilse.

"You see," she explains, "there is for the moment no possibility of coming to Paris. You would not get a visa and you would not get an allowance to stay here. You must understand that there are new war regulations about strangers staying in Paris. And I really do not think you would like it very much having to stay home from six o'clock in the evening because of the blackout."

Hulda suggests that Ilse writes to Irma Lange who might be able to help and gives her address as 4 Selcroft Road, Dunn Purley in Surrey.

Ilse and Roman are having problems communicating and Hulda suggests that Ilse writes a letter to Roman and sends it to her in Paris.

"Do not mention his name," she instructs Ilse, "and at the end only put your initials not your full name. I will send this letter to Grandma via Budapest because I regularly get letters from Grandma through Mr Kun in Budapest. They go much quicker and safer than via Anni in Rotterdam."

She tells Ilse that she is very grateful to Anni who has arranged to send money to Gisela in Vienna and has also sent her food parcels. She ends by asking Ilse again what happened between her and her father to make them fall out.[144]

*

Hulda's last letter in October gives a further insight into how precarious life was for Jewish refugees in Paris at that time.

---

[144]  Letter dated 22 October 1939 from Hulda Frankenbusch to Ilse Frankenbusch.

'Yesterday," she says, "Dr Kris came home from the concentration camp where he had been for more than six weeks. He was sent home because he fell and broke his arm. He looked like a soldier returning from the Russian war: dirty, unshaven and stern. Mr Recht, who was also in a camp, is now in Hospital with lung disease. His wife is allowed to visit him once a day for ten minutes and I have also been once to see him."

Everyone Hulda knows is rather miserable at the moment but she is trying to make the best of things. She went to the local theatre in the same street as her hotel.

"They were performing four little comedies by Sasha Guitry," she tells Ilse, "with him as the leading actor and his present wife and divorced wife acting with him – so you can imagine!" she says.

"On Sunday mornings," she also says, "I very often go to the Madeleine church – they have such very good music there. Today they performed a masse and Mozart's Ave Verum which I enjoyed very much."

"Music is something which always helps me get through the bad times," she writes.[145]

*

In October, the HMS Royal Oak was sunk by a German U-boat in Scapa Flow in the Orkneys and it was Hoy in the Orkneys where the first bomb to land in the UK exploded. Scapa Flow was established as one of the main British naval bases during both world wars and was built to prevent access to the North Sea. The first enemy aircraft, a Junkers Ju 88, was brought down by Spitfires of the RAF Fighter Command following an attack on Rosyth Naval Dockyard in Scotland.[146]

Systematic mass deportations of the Viennese Jewish population began on 20 October 1939 when, on Eichmann's orders, SS and police officials deported 1,500 Jews from Vienna to a camp in Nisko, Poland.[147]

---

[145] Letter dated 29 October 1939 from Hulda Frankenbusch to Ilse Frankenbusch.
[146] Wikipedia. Op.cit. Footnote 131.
[147] United States Holocaust Memorial Museum. Holocaust Encyclopedia. Vienna. http://www.ushmm.org/wlc/en/article.php?ModuleId=10005452. Accessed 13 February 2013.

*

Hulda wrote to Ilse with birthday wishes for 9 November 1939, Ilse's 24th birthday.

"There are so many things I would like to tell you," says Hulda, "but mainly that I want to see you in the future happy and lucky and content and as sweet and loving as I always knew you." She also sends her two pounds for her birthday and a few lines that Roman has added to a letter she has received from Gisela.[148]

A few days later Hulda received a certificate from the consular section of the Czechoslovakian Legation in Paris confirming that she was recognised as a Czechoslovakian national.[149]

Ten days later Ilse is no longer living or working with her father in Birmingham and has moved down to Surrey. Irma Lange apparently helped Ilse find somewhere to live and for this Hulda is very grateful and sends her best wishes and greetings to Irma. Hulda wants to know all about Ilse's new place and where Irma is living and whether her son Hanns is with her. She asks whether Ilse has received the two letters she sent to the Birmingham address.

'You never can tell," she says, "what your father will do with the letters and the money." She obviously does not entirely trust her former husband.

She asks whether Ilse took all her luggage with her, whether Hansi is still in Bournemouth and has heard from Rudi. Hulda has heard from Gisela who says that she and Roman have both heard from Ilse. She adds a handwritten note at the bottom of the postcard:

"Four o'clock in the morning and I am sitting in the cellar – I wish they would let me go to sleep again!"

The postcard is addressed to Ilse , c/o Mrs Heaton-Smith, Yateley House, Godstone Road, Kenley, Surrey.[150]

*

---

[148] Letter dated 3 November 1939 from Hulda Frankenbusch to Ilse Frankenbusch.
[149] Letter dated 7 November 1939 from the first Secretary of the Czechoslovakian Legation to Hulda Frankenbusch.
[150] Letter dated 12 November 1939 from Hulda Frankenbusch to Ilse Frankenbusch.

A week later and Hulda has heard from Ilse again and it seems that she is content, the people she is working for are kind and she lives close to Irma so isn't so alone. Hulda wants to know if Kenley is a town and what it is like, whether there are any children in the household or just the doctor and his wife. She also wants to know if there are servants in the household and asks after Hanns, Irma's son and whether he is working.

Ilse has had a letter from Roman and Sani has written to Hulda to tell her he has sent a food parcel of butter and bacon to Gisela in Vienna.

"I hope she will get it" says Hulda, "But isn't this kind of him?"

Hulda tells Ilse that the 'affair' with her luggage has been resolved.

All five pieces are free and safe in storage where they will cost her 25 Francs a month. The whole business cost her 1200 Francs, half of it already paid and the other half to be paid in January.

"I am really curious about when and where I will unpack these trunks," she says, "but I am glad it's all over as it was a rather complicated affair."

After saying that there was nothing new to report from Paris, she remembers something she was going to tell Ilse.

"The biggest sensation of last week," she says, "was the English soldiers marching into Paris to the tune of the Lambeth Walk!"[151]

*

The last letter of November from Hulda encloses a letter from Roman which was sent from Sani. Hulda suggests that Ilse writes directly to Sani just as Hulda does and gives his address: Alexander Torday, *Fery Oszkar* u.35b, Budapest, Hungary, via Italia. Hulda says that the 'via Italia' part is very important. Both Gisela and Anni have complained that they haven't heard from Hulda recently so it seems that letters sent via Holland aren't getting through so she suggests that it's probably best to write only to Sani. Anni has also written that Wim's grandfather has died and suggests to Ilse that she might like to write a few lines of condolence on behalf of the family.

---

[151] Letter dated 19 November 1939 from Hulda Frankenbusch to Ilse Frankenbusch.

A handwritten note at the bottom of the letter gives the address of Dr. Kris' daughter, Mia. She is in a convent: St Joseph's Priory, Harrow Road West, Dorking, Surrey. Hulda suggests to Ilse that if it isn't too far away, she could go and see her.[152]

*

Hulda's last two letters for the year are rather sad because Christmas is looming and she will be spending it alone. On Christmas Eve she has been invited to the Recht's but there are very few public festivities this year and she will have to get home early before the Metro closes as she daren't walk the streets during the blackout. She is anxious about Anni as she has had very little news from her.

"What you read in the newspapers about her country," Hulda says, "is not very encouraging."[153]

*My dear girl,*
        *I received your card from the 7.inst.*
*I am glad you are well and not unsatisfied with*
*your work.Will you have guests for Christmass to?*
*In ten days...o,darling,I will be so lonely this*
*year!On Christmass-eve I am invited at Rechts..did*
*I write you that he is back from the Camp,but rather*
*sick and worn out.There is no"reveillen"this year*
*and I will hurry to get home early,as long as the MM*
*Metro is going,because I cannot walk in the street*
*in this darkness.....It would be nice,if this Mr.*
*Wildshut would come to see me.Did you give him my*
*new adress?And did you see him this last weeks?*
*I am rather anxious about Anni.It is now rather*
*an long time,that I had no news from her and what*
*you read in the news'papers about her country,is*

*Hulda's Christmas postcard to Ilse December 1939*

[152]   Letter dated 30 November 1939 from Hulda Frankenbusch to Ilse Frankenbusch.
[153]   Postcard dated 14 December 1939 from Hulda Frankenbusch to Ilse Frankenbusch.

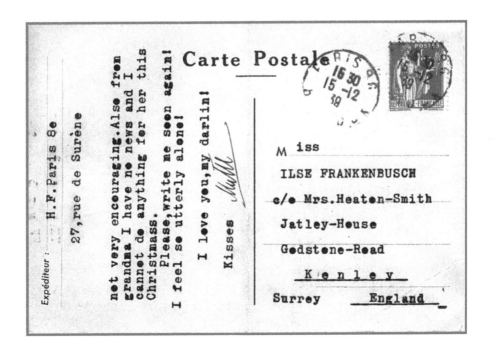

Carte Postale

Expéditeur : H.F.Paris 8e  
27,rue de Surène

not very encouraging.Also from  
grandma I have no news and I  
cannot do anything for her this  
Christmass.  
Please,write me soon again!  
I feel so utterly alone!

I love you,my darlin!  
Kisses

Miss  
ILSE FRANKENBUSCH  
c/o Mrs.Heaton-Smith  
Jatley-House  
Godstone-Road  
K e n l e y  
Surrey        England

A week before Christmas Hulda writes again to wish Ilse a good Christmas holiday and to send her a small Christmas parcel. Her main news is that she has had a letter from Gisela who wrote to tell her that Aunt Julia Squarenina is in the Rothschild Hospital and is very sick and that Aunt Gisa Miskoloczy (Julia's sister) has come to Vienna to visit her. Roman brought Aunt Gisa to have tea with grandma and afterwards took her home. Aunt Gisa could tell grandma everything about Kenley in Surrey because Irma's husband knew it well through Irma's descriptions.

"I can imagine them," says Hulda, "sitting together and talking and talking about us poor lonely children!"

She ends by saying that all her thoughts will be with Ilse on Christmas Day.[154]

*

By the end of 1939, after a quick campaign in the east, the war along the Franco-German frontier had settled into a largely non-

---

[154] Letter dated 18 December 1939 from Hulda Frankenbusch to Ilse Frankenbusch.

confrontational period which became known as the Phoney War. The Soviet Union wanted to annex Finland and offered a union agreement which was rejected. This caused the Soviets to attack Finland on 30 November 1939 and thus started the Winter War which was to continue for three months.[155] On 13 December 1939 the Battle of the River Plate took place off the coasts of Argentina and Uruguay in South America between HMS Exeter, HMS Ajax and HMNZS Achilles and the German cruiser *Admiral Graf Spee* forcing the latter to scuttle herself four days later. A day after this RAF Bomber Command, on a daylight mission to attack *Kriegsmarine* ships in the Heligoland Bight off the North Sea coast of Germany, is repulsed by *Luftwaffe* fighter aircraft.[156]

In Vienna Eichmann had informed the leaders of the Jewish community that all Jews who did not emigrate within a year would be exiled to occupied Poland. During the first four months of the war, another 11,000 Jews had succeeded in emigrating to neutral countries. Of the 53,400 people still registered with the Viennese Jewish community at the end of 1939, 45,000 were dependent on social welfare. However, the community continued to arrange training in preparation for emigration and over 5,000 children of school age continued to study in its 14 educational institutions. Among the community's projected plans for 1940 was its own gradual dissolution, so that, by the end of that year, its only duty would be the care of 24,000 aged and infirm who would be unable to emigrate.[157]

*

For the three women, the end of 1939 brought with it the end of any hope of being together again in the near future. Europe was at war, borders were closed and travel between enemy countries was impossible. Most countries were on a war footing with formerly unknown restrictions on personal life including such things as ID cards, conscription, blackouts, food rationing and permits for domestic travel. In France and England there was an insidious fear of 'foreigners', people who were 'different', and this suspicion made for

---

[155]  Wikipedia. European Theatre of World War II.
      http://en.wikipedia.org/wiki/European_Theatre_of_World_War_II . Accessed 26 April 2013.
[156]  Wikipedia, Op.cit. footnote 131.
[157]  Encyclpaedia Judaica. Op.cit. footnote 140.

an uncomfortable co-existence between long-time residents and refugees. In the German Reich, it was simply being a Jew that created the fear.

For the foreseeable future, Gisela, Hulda and Ilse were each condemned to a life alone in a world that had changed forever. Their separate worlds were ones of increasing isolation, fear for the future and the only hope left to them was a simple hope for survival. All they could do was stay quiet in their lonely worlds and aim to survive whatever the world threw at them.

The Viennese philosopher, David Oppenheim, also trapped in the city at the end of 1939, wrote the following:

"Now world history is marching at the double ... the scales on which the fate of peoples is weighed are tilting and the will of the individual cannot change this by a hair's breadth. One can only observe it, and prepare oneself not to be totally at a loss whichever way the decision goes."[158]

---

[158]  Singer, Peter. Pushing time away: my grandfather and the tragedy of Jewish Vienna. London, Granta Publications, 2003. p.206.

# Chapter 6

**1940**

**January**

**to**

**May**

The winter of 1939 – 40 was a particularly bad one across the length and breadth of Europe. There was more snow than usual in Vienna and ice storms of freezing rain across northern Europe.

Hulda started off the year confined to bed with a bad cold in her first letter of the year.[159] This had developed into flu by the time she wrote her second letter. The mail service seems to be breaking down as, in her first letter, she has not yet received the Christmas parcels that Anni and Ilse have sent and in the second letter she says that only the parcel from Anni has arrived. However, she is glad to hear that Ilse is happy at Irma's, gets spoilt a bit and has her cousin Hanns, someone of her own age, as company.

While she had flu the cleaning lady looked after her but charged her Frs.11.25 for soup and a meat dish!

"For that price,' says Hulda, "I could eat out with starters, desert, wine and bread!"

As usual Hulda is concerned about money and says that because she has to send Gisela's 'pension' through Anni's bank, it now costs her Frs 250 more than before. Still she is glad that it happens at all.

'After all," she writes, "what would grandmother do if all possibilities were cut off."[160]

*

Mid-January and it is still bitterly cold. Hulda says she is freezing, still feeling ill and suffering badly from the cold. She has had a letter from Gisela who told her that Roman's brother, Karl, is getting married this month but no-one is impressed with his bride, Martha. She asks where Hansi is as even her parents haven't heard from her. Apparently Rudi did a concert in Rio but hasn't been in touch with anyone and Hulda asks whether Ilse has any news of him.

Apart from feeling sick Hulda also has a new neighbor who has a radio as well as a gramophone and plays them alternately.

"I think she will annoy me," says Hulda, "and on top of it she's German! I don't think I can bear it! She got the radio as a new year's present so this disturbance is very new! Urgh!!!"

---

[159]  Letter dated 3 January 1940 from Hulda Frankenbusch to Ilse Frankenbusch.
[160]  Letter dated 8 January 1940 from Hulda Frankenbusch to Ilse Frankenbusch.

Hulda is not very happy![161]

*

In the next letter, it is still freezing and she is still ill – she had a migraine for ten hours the day before and couldn't eat anything because it came straight back up again. Today she is feeling better but still not able to eat much. She believes that it is the harsh winter that has made her so sick.

"It's always cloudy and there's no sun," she says. "I really need a change."

However, she has at last heard from Ilse even though the Christmas parcel still hasn't arrived. It seems Ilse has told her that she sent her a pair of gloves and Hulda comments that it's a pity they got lost because she needed them.

With this letter she is enclosing four letters, two from Sani to Hulda, one from Roman to Hulda and one from Gisela to Sani – it seems that letters are shared around as very precious commodities. Hulda reminds Ilse that it is Gisela's birthday on 11 February and tells her that she has ordered a food parcel for Gisela from Sani and Anni as that is what she needs most right now.

Hulda has been communicating with Irma about sending money to Gisela and it seems that Aunt Gisa Miskolczy has been talking to Walter, Irma's husband, about the same thing. The extended family are rallying round and putting measures in place to make sure that Gisela has the financial support she needs to make her life as comfortable as possible in these uncertain times.

Dr and Frau Kris came to see her the previous day and though it was very nice of them Hulda says, being around them makes her nervous since Dr Kris returned from the interment camp

"I can tell you," she says, "When I leave here it will be good to get away from this immigrant society."[162]

*

---

[161]  Letter dated 13 January 1940 from Hulda Frankenbusch to Ilse Frankenbusch.
[162]  Letter dated 24 January 1940 from Hulda Frankenbusch to Ilse Frankenbusch.

From Hulda's next letter, it sounds as if Ilse has told her mother in no uncertain terms, that if she is so unhappy in Paris and has been talking about leaving for several months, then maybe it was time to do something about it. Obviously the weather doesn't suit her, but neither does the 'hurly-burly' of the city, nor being surrounded by an immigrant population. Now that she knows for certain that Gisela won't be able to join her she is, once again, a free agent – or as free as it is possible to be in a country at war. There is no knowing how long the war will last and it is important that her living conditions should be as comfortable as possible in order to sit it out and wait for better times when they can all be together again. Gisela's welfare has been taken care of with the help of the extended family, Ilse's life in England seems to have settled down, Anni has Wim to take care of her so now it's time for Hulda to look after herself.

As we don't have Ilse's letter, this is all conjecture but it is the kind of thing my mother would have said.

Hulda replies with surprise at Ilse's 'strong letter' but has taken immediate action. She went to see 'good old Mr Wynn" at Morgan Bank and he told her what she needed to do, but warned her that it would take 10-14 days to sort out. Tomorrow she is going to the police to start the process of getting a travel permit. It's not certain that she'll get one but

"as a Czech with good bank guarantees and good references," she says, "I may have an advantage."

Ilse must have sent Hulda a cheque through the doctor, her employer, because Hulda mentions that she is having trouble cashing it and the bank is asking for confirmation from the doctor that he gave permission to send the money abroad. In the meantime, the bank is holding on to the cheque.

The weather has changed and it is not so cold any more.

"But," she says, "instead it is raining non-stop and you totally forget what Paris looks like in the sun!" [163]

\*

At last Ilse's Christmas parcel has arrived and now Hulda has two pairs of gloves! The parcel was mailed in England on 6 December

---

[163] Letter dated 1 February 1940 from Hulda Frankenbusch to Ilse Frankenbusch.

1939 and arrived in Paris the first week in February 1940. Hulda mentions that a letter from Gisela mailed on 20 January, arrived on 1 February and another mailed on 17 January arrived on 5 February. She has had nothing from Anni since December.

"The post is very puzzling," says Hulda.

The cheque issue from the previous letter is still sorting itself out but it seems that Ilse must have sent it to help with Hulda's travel expenses when she leaves Paris.

"I just hope I get the travel permit," Hulda says, "because if it doesn't work out you'll get the money back – after all, there's no point in having travel money if I can't travel."

"I want some sun!" she writes, "My bronchial catarrh and my cough are annoying me – what use are medicines, when all I need is sun!"[164]

*

In her next letter Hulda is still waiting for her travel permit.

"The authority," she writes, "says I should get it and the police are sceptical. But as neither of these make the decision and it's the military that have the responsibility, these opinions shouldn't matter."

She had another tooth out the previous day and came straight home and went to bed. She still has a 'fat cheek' but is feeling better.

Robert has written his second letter from Algiers [he volunteered for the French Foreign Legion in late 1939]. He hasn't heard from his sister Greta but otherwise seems happy.

"At least he has some sun!" says Hulda, "I'm jealous of him! He spoke of palm trees and sunsets during the journey."

She has also heard from Sani who has sent Gisela another food parcel for her birthday.

"He is really good!" says Hulda.[165]

*

---

[164] Letter dated 8 February 1940 from Hulda Frankenbusch to Ilse Frankenbusch.
[165] Letter dated 13 February 1940 from Hulda Frankenbusch to Ilse Frankenbusch.

In her last letter of February she says "As you can see I am still in Paris". Two days earlier she had been to see the authorities about her travel permit and they had laughed at her because she had only waited ten days and other people have had to wait for more than four weeks.

"You must understand," she writes, "that the French authorities have a very different way of dealing with foreigners than the English do. Here we are all refugees, which more or less means criminals!"

She is also treading carefully in her dealings with the authorities because she has now been in France for 18 months and if, after the war ends, she has been there for three uninterrupted years, then she would be eligible for French citizenship. As no-one knows what is going to happen to Czechoslovakia, she doesn't want to ruin her chances in France.

"France and the French people as such are really very nice," she comments, "and it is surely preferable to other European countries."

It sounds like Ilse wants her to try and get a travel permit to England, but Hulda suggests that Ilse should try and come to her in France. She doesn't think she'd have enough money to live on in England and doesn't think she'd be able to get a job.

In return for Ilse's gifts to her, she is sending her daughter a parcel by the same post as this letter – a pair of gloves which Gisela had sent her but which are too big for her, and two scarves, one silk and one wool which she bought in the sales.[166]

*

On 24 February Hulda hears from the Military Department of the National Czechoslovakian Committee which states that they do not have any objections to her travelling to Nice from Paris and confirms that she is the holder of Czecholslovakian passport no.16537 issued on 17 November 1932 by the Consulate of the Republic of Czechoslovakia in Vienna.

This would be one of the documents she had been waiting patiently for and would take her one step closer to leaving Paris.

---

[166] Letter dated 21 February 1940 from Hulda Frankenbusch to Ilse Frankenbusch.

The next letter was to Irma Lange in London and announces that she has got her travel permit and hopefully will be travelling to Nice on Friday 8 March.

NARODNI VYBOR CESKOSLOVENSKY/COPIE!
    Vojenska Sprava
    . . . . . . . . . . .

COMITE NATIONAL TCHECOSLOVAQUE
DEPARTEMENT MILITAIRE.


        N§ 3326/40


            A T T E S T A T I O N
            ------------------------------

            Le Comité National Tchécoslovaque-Département Militaire-

    certifie qu'il n'a pas d'objection au voyage de Paris à Nice et

    retour de Madame F r a n k e n b u s c h-ova Hulda né le 19 Mai RMMDM

    1890 à Vienne titulaire du passeport tchécoslovaque N§ 16537 émis

    le 17 Novembre 1932 par le Consulat Général de la République

    Tchécoslovaque à Vienne.


                        Paris, le 24 Février 1940

*Hulda's travel permit from the*
*Czech Military Dept, Paris, Feb.1940.*


"I can't wait," she says, "because it is really cold here again and I'd like a bit of warmth. I assume that it's already spring-like in the south because here they are already selling Nice violets."

She tells Irma that she has sent off to her the money for February and will wait to hear that it has arrived before sending the money for March. This is the money that Hulda sends monthly to Irma in exchange for the same amount being sent to Gisela by Walter, Irma's husband, who is still in the Reich. Hulda needs to know first that the payment system is working properly.[167]

*

By the beginning of March the Winter War between the Soviet Union and Finland was drawing to a close and other countries in Scandinavia

---

[167] Letter dated 2 March 1940 from Hulda Frankenbusch to Irma Lange.

128

were being drawn into the war with Germany. On 1 March 1940 Hitler issued the order for the invasion and occupation of Norway and Denmark under the code word *Weserubung.*

Hitler had long realized that the occupation of Norway was crucial in his long-term plans for Europe. The control of Norway's extensive coastline was considered extremely important in the battle for the North Sea and would provide an alternative means of access for German warships and submarines into the Atlantic. Also, the continuing supply of Sweden's iron ore was important for Germany's war effort. Nine million tons of this came from northern Sweden and was shipped to Germany via the port of Lulea. However Lulea freezes over during the winter months whereas the Norwegian port of Narvik does not. Therefore the control of Narvik would have been essential if Germany wanted to guarantee the continued movement of iron ore from Sweden.

The British government was equally aware of the strategic importance of Norway and as early as 19 September 1939, Churchill had told Cabinet that the German transportations of iron ore had to be stopped. He proposed that the waters around Narvik should be mined but Cabinet didn't support this as they were wary of breaching Norway's neutrality.[168]

Having maintained its neutrality during World War I, Norway wanted to continue on this path on the assumption that there would be no need to bring Norway into a war if she remained neutral. Above all else, Norway didn't want to be at war with the United Kingdom. By late 1939, there was an increasing sense of urgency in Norway that there was a need to prepare, not only to protect its neutrality, but also to fight for its freedom and independence. Efforts to improve its military readiness and capability continued between September 1939 and April 1940 to the extent that the Norwegian parliament even assumed a national debt.

Norway managed to negotiate favourable trade treaties both with the United Kingdom and with Germany at this time but it became increasingly clear that both countries had a strategic interest in denying

---

[168]  History Learning Site. The invasion of Norway 1940. http://www.historylearningsite.co.uk/invasion_of_norway_1940.htm. Accessed 7 May 2013.

the other access to Norway. It was only a matter of time before Norway's neutrality was seriously challenged.[169]

*

Hulda arrives in Nice on 9 March 1940.

Her last letter to Ilse from Paris had outlined her journey – she was leaving on 8 March at 8pm and would arrive in Nice at 11am the next day. She is looking forward to it and is very happy to be going. She didn't have an address to go to but was sure she'd be able to find a room somewhere. In the meantime she suggested that if Ilse wanted to write she could address a letter to the *Poste Cenrale*, Nice, Alpes-Maritime, until Hulda lets her know her new address.

She'd found the *pension* she was staying in by looking at the adverts at the railway station and had chosen it because it was in a nice area and not too far from the sea.. She had decided to give it a try and if it didn't work out then she could always find somewhere else later on.

---

[169]   Wikipedia. Occupation of Norway by Nazi Germany.
   http://en.wikipedia.org/wiki/Occupation_of_Norway_by_Nazi_Germany.
   Accessed 7 May 2013.

*Hulda's postcard to Ilse on arrival in Nice, March 1940.*

When she arrived in Nice all she'd wanted was somewhere to lay her head and recover from the journey and the stressful times in Paris leading up to that exciting moment when she finally stepped onto the train and knew she was on her way. Her first note to Ilse from Nice gives the new address – *Pension Dufaur*, 59 *Boulevard Victor Hugo* which she said wasn't very nice but was in a nice street and not too expensive.

"I am in Nice,' she says, "and it is a dream! Lovely![170]

\*

Immediately after breakfast at the *pension*, she put on her coat, gathered up her bag and stepped out the door – into glorious sunshine – such a change from the grey chill of a Parisian winter. It was so wonderful to see the sun despite the brisk March air – it was a truly beautiful spring day and her spirits lifted. She turned right out of the door of the *pension* and walked to the first turning and turned left towards the sea which she could see at the end of the road. At the bottom of the street, she turned left and headed along the *Promenade des Anglais* towards the center of Nice and the old town.

---

[170] Postcard dated 12 March 1940 from Hulda Frankrnbusch to Ilse Frankenbusch.

The blue sky and sea immediately reminded her of Abbazzia and Sani's villa there where she, Gisela and Ilse had often gone to stay whenever they could manage some time away from Vienna.

"But it is more beautiful and magnificent," she says, "because the view of the sea is not so narrow and the surroundings are much more beautiful."[171]

The coast was completely different of course with Abbazia having a wild rocky shoreline and Nice having a long pebble beach and gently rolling waves lapping the shore. However, the colours were the same – the brightness of the blue sky and sea, the greens of the lush vegetation and the pinks, blues, yellows and violets of the flowers in the many parks – even now in mid-March.

"Nice is beautiful! Dreamlike!" writes Hulda, "The sun is shining, the sea is blue and I have seen the first orange trees ... and palm trees ... and laurel ... and cactuses!!"[172]

Hulda wandered on up the *Promenade des Anglais,* so named because it was paid for by Nice's English colony in 1822[173]. It was developed as a shore side strolling path and was a good way to get an idea of the layout of the town as well as revel in the beauty of the sea view along the *Baie des Anges.* She had her Baedecker with her and as she walked on she noticed the magnificent façade of the palace built for the Romanian Henri Negresco in 1912 and the art deco *Palais de la Mediterranee* , the property of American millionaire Frank Jay Gould and the home of Nice's Hotel-Casino[174].

Moving east towards the old town, the Promenade became the *Quai des Etaats-Unis,* named after the United States as a memorial to President Wilson's decision in 1917 to join WWI. Hulda stopped to look at the memorial honouring the 4000 *Nicois* who died in WWI, which was carved into the rock at the quay's eastern end[175]. As she looked she couldn't help but wonder what the future would bring as the conflict that had started six months ago crept closer and closer to France. However it was a beautiful day and she was feeling optimistic

---

[171] Letter dated 16 March 1940 from Hulda Frankenbusch to Ilse Frankenbusch.
[172] Ibid. footnote 13.
[173] Edwards, Natasha. Nice, Cannes and Monte Carlo: Berlitz pocket guide. Singapore, Berlitz Publishing, 2009. p.38
[174] Ibid. footnote 173 p.39.
[175] Ibid. footnote 173 p.32.

so she decided it was impossible to believe that war could possibly come to this south-eastern corner of France.

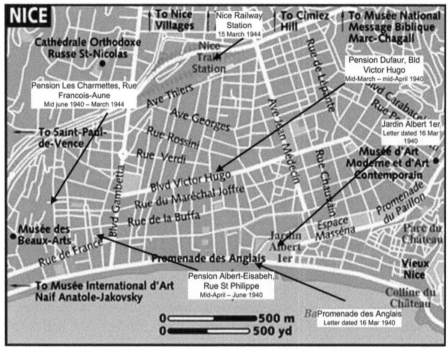

*Hulda's Nice, March 1940 – March 1944*

She decided she'd walked far enough for one day so turned round and returned to the *Jardin Albert I* first developed in the 19<sup>th</sup> century[176]. She found a seat in the sun and sat down and took her Baedeker out so that she could at least look as if she was reading while she watched the people strolling around in the park. They seemed a lot more relaxed than the Parisians, without the feeling of anxiety and worry about the future that had made living in Paris so stressful – never knowing whom you could trust or when another acquaintance would disappear[177].

"Here we are far away from the action," she writes to Ilse, "and if it wasn't for all the uniforms, you'd think you were in total freedom."[178]

[176] Ibid. footnote 173 p.35.
[177] Letters dated 3 September 1939 and 29 October 1939 from Hulda Frankenbusch to Ilse Frankebusch.
[178] Frankenbusch, Hulda. Op.cit. footnote 171.

133

After a rest in the gardens she decided to walk up to the shops in the *Avenue Jean Medecin* and look for a small Easter gift for Ilse. She'd already bought a small flower brooch from Paris but thought something from Nice would mark the season as an extra special one[179]. She settled on a small basket of candied fruit, a speciality of Nice and once that was done, she treated herself to a coffee and cake in one of the many cafes. Once again it was a joy to be able to sit outside and feel comfortable and hopeful about the future.

At this rate, with all the walking and the fresh air she would soon be feeling a lot better and the coughs and headaches she'd developed in Paris would be things of the past.

"I am taking long walks," she writes, "but am being very careful because I'm still coughing nicely. But because of the sun I'll soon feel very well."[180]

That afternoon Hulda sits in her room and writes to Ilse, describing her pension.

"My room is high up and big," she says, "but a bit shabby though I have asked for several improvements and they have been done. It reminds me of soulful remembrances – decent but old and a bit shabby."[181]

While she was writing to Ilse, it was like having her there in the room and talking to her and for a short time she could forget her loneliness and concentrate on her beloved daughter.


She tells her about the other people in the pension. There are 28 people including herself. There are two German couples with their entire families, a few French officer's wives whose husbands were only there at the weekends, a Dutch lady and two English ladies.

"So," says Hulda, "it's richly international!"

"The place," she says, "is several centuries old, in fact stone age ... very much like in Baden."

---

[179] Frankenbusch, Hulda. Op.cit. footnote 171.
[180] Frankenbusch, Hulda. Op.cit. footnote 117.
[181] Frankenbusch, Hulda. Op.cit. footnote 171.

Then she mentions the people who work there. Firstly, an old lady and her daughter (who looks like a film diva) – both very nice. Then, a 'room governess' whose mother looks after the washing and also a cook, a kitchen assistant and two chambermaids. All that for 28 people, she said, and it doesn't work.

"Organisation of a dog!" she comments.

The food was the weak point, she said and from next week she was going to go to half-board instead of full-board and that would save her 9Frs. The food was not particularly good and definitely not enough for what she was paying – 38Frs for full board. Last night's meal was a potato soup, minced fish with mussels in a gratinee, casserole and two tiny hams.

"What an interesting combination," she comments.

At midday they eat meat – and it's never cooked right, she writes. In the evenings, only twelve people eat in and there are four people to serve them. She tells Ilse that in the kitchen they all scream at each other as if they had to cook for 80 people. Having managed a similar boarding house in Baden, Hulda finds it all very amusing.

"I find it very funny," she says, "and I only wish some of our old ladies [from Baden] could be here to learn some modesty."

"People here put up with anything and don't complain," she writes, "and of course, as a foreigner, I'm polite and don't say anything."

As usual, Hulda was worried about money and was wondering if the transfer from Paris would work. She told Ilse that the journey was very expensive and it was only thanks to the £4 that Ilse had sent her that she was able to travel at all. So, for that, she was very grateful because she was very, very happy to be here.[182]

She ended her letter, folded it, put it in an envelope, addressed it and sealed it. Tomorrow she would go to the post office and buy the stamps and mail it.

The next letter was written on Easter Sunday and she hadn't heard from Ilse and was feeling a bit lonely. She was having problems sending money abroad and had been told that from now on she needs a permit. She knows where to go to get it but can't do anything about it

---

[182] Frankenbusch, Hulda. Op.cit. footnote 171.

until after Easter. In the meantime she asks Ilse to let Irma know why she cannot send her any money at the moment.

She tells Ilse how she had spent Easter – she had eaten 'stone-hard chicken' on the promenade and had gone to the Casino-Bar in the evening. Really boring, she said, and even the weather left a lot to be desired but it was still a lot better than in Paris.

"Here I feel a lot more at ease and freer, and," she adds, "there are no blackouts at all in the evening."

Her gasmask is still in her suitcase and if she really tries she can imagine that the war was just a bad dream.

"Hopefully it will stay that way here." she writes.

Her health has improved a lot and the breathing problems she had in Paris have completely disappeared in the sea air. Until she got to Nice she hadn't realized how bad the air had been in Paris.

"I've even caught the sun a bit," she writes, "because I have tried to make my freckles grow so that I don't become a pasty-face again."

She says that when you're about to turn 50 you have to become sensible and reminds Ilse that it will be her 50th birthday in May.

"Ha ha!" she comments, "who isn't laughing?!"[183]

\*

The next time she writes she has received a card as well as a letter from Ilse both of which took seven days to reach her – they'll both have to have a lot of patience, she says. Ilse hasn't mentioned the Easter letter Hulda wrote or the Easter parcel she sent so she wonders if they arrived.

Everything is going well and she describes her life in Nice.

"The weather is wonderful," she says, "sea and sky are blue, the sun is shining, the mimosas are blossoming and the lemon and orange trees already have fat fruits. Nice's surroundings are wonderful and I take long walks over the hills and in the olive groves! It is often dreamily beautiful! In the evenings I often sit in a small but very nice beach bar that is built right in the sea so that all you can see around you is dark blue water."

---

[183] Letter dated 24 March 1940 from Hulda Frankenbusch to Ilse Frankenbusch.

Many people are already swimming in early April and she'd like to join them but the doctor says to wait until at least mid-May.

Hulda plans to stay for the summer, has found a nicer and cheaper place to live and will move in next Monday. It is a nice quiet villa with a garden that has been taken over by the daughter of her present landlady. She will have a first floor room with quite a large balcony overlooking the garden. The room itself is smaller than the one she's in at the moment but it's nicely decorated and has hot and cold running water. The present one has only cold water and the warm water is brought up to you in buckets. She has decided to go with full board again as it seems to work out cheaper in the long run but this time she will only be paying Frs 33 so will save Frs 5 on what she is paying now. The best thing is that in her new place she won't be surrounded by a load of old ladies – that could get quite depressing at times. Her new address will be *Pension Albert-Elisabeth*, 39 *Rue St-Philippe* and she'll be a lot closer to the beach and the swimming pool than she is now.

"I can't wait to get in the water," she says, "but before that I'm going to lie on my balcony and rub cream in so that I won't be too pale when I go to the pool."

She is still worried about money as she only has enough left for one week. Hopefully the money from Morgan Bank will arrive soon so that with that and what she'll save on her lodgings, she'll be able to pay off her debts during the rest of April and May. She should hear soon that her application for the permit to send money abroad has been successful and then she will be able to send money to Irma again.

She mentions that she has had a card from the Herzels who are well, also a letter from Robert and reminds Ilse that it is Anni's 30th birthday on the 9th of the month.[184]

*

On Anni's 30th birthday, the 9 April 1940, the invasion of Norway began. German warships entered major Norwegian ports from Narvik to Oslo deploying thousands of troops while major airfields were attacked by air and by parachutists. At the same time German troops occupied Copenhagen and other Danish cities while the northern

---

[184] Letter dated 2 April from Hulda Frankenbusch to Ilse Frankenbusch.

airfields, strategically essential as a bridge to Norway, were taken by parachutists.

Denmark fell quickly to a vastly superior military force and, to avoid further bloodshed, King Christian X surrendered almost immediately.

German warships were able to move into the Norwegian ports because local garrisons were ordered to allow the Germans to land unopposed. The order came from a Norwegian commander loyal to Norway's pro-fascist former Foreign Minister, Vidkun Quisling. In Oslo, the occupation of Norway began with the establishment of a puppet government led by Quisling. Norwegian troops refused to recognize German rule in the guise of the Quisling government and continued to fight alongside British troops for a further two months – thus making Norway the nation that withstood a German invasion for the longest period of time, aside from the Soviet Union.[185]

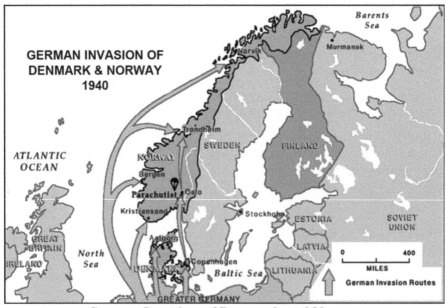

*German Invasion of Denmark and Norway*

\*

[185]   This day in history. April 9. http://www.history.com/this-day-in-history/germany-invades-norway-and-denmark. Accessed 7 May 2013.

By mid April Ilse has written to say she has been to visit Hansi, has really enjoyed visiting a new place and has come home happy.

"Did we ever think we'd get to know so much of the world?" Hulda comments, "And today we still don't know where destiny will take us? Let's hope for the best and hope it won't be bad."

Ilse has obviously proposed a visit to her mother.

Hulda says excitedly, "The idea that you may be able to come here makes me all dizzy!"

Hulda immediately starts planning and giving Ilse lots of advice.

"It would be good if you could forward your receipt from Paris," she says, "that shows that we paid Frs 400 for a stay there without you staying. Maybe that will help you visit your mother. The following facts are useful: your mother, who has lived in France since October 1938 and has an ID card No EK 48889, which is valid until October 1941, receives a pension of $70 per month, deposited by Madame Princess Margaret D Boncompagni (now in Washington USA) and paid by the Bank Morgan & Co, Paris, 14 *Place Vendome*. For my travel to Nice, I needed proof of Loyalty, which the Czech Consulate provided and also a permit from the Czech Army Commando."

She says she is sending copies of both these documents and urges Ilse to take these documents to the Czech Consulate in London as soon as possible and not to leave it to the last minute as everything takes longer than anyone could imagine. However Ilse's situation is different from Hulda's as she will probably only apply for a short period whereas Hulda applied for three months originally and is now applying to stay longer.

She then goes on to talk about the costs of living in Nice.

"The costs of staying here aren't really that large. You can live in my room and then the costs won't be more than Frs 30 per day all inclusive. So for one week that's Frs 210 – calculate another half of that for extra spending – with Frs 15 here each day you can do a lot, cinemas, music cafes, casino – whatever you want – so together that would be Frs 315 for a week. Since £1 is now worth Frs 178.50, it will cost less than £2. If you took £2 or £3 with you, you could buy all sorts. Now you can see why I want to stay here!"

She expresses the hope that God likes her just a little bit and will let her stay here in the sun and won't send any more complications that will take her away from Nice.

"However," she says, "Nowadays we don't know anything for sure!"

She tells Ilse that she visited the Schafer daughters in Cannes the day before and says they are paying Frs 45 per day for their lodgings and it's not as nice as where she is. She says that Cannes is a lot more expensive than Nice, the people may be more elegant but life seems a lot more boring. The bus journey to Cannes was 1½ hours, only cost Frs 16 return and was most interesting and beautiful.

She also says that Sani is now in Geneva and hoping to go to Amsterdam and visit Anni while he is in Holland. Hulda has written to Anni but hasn't had a reply and is worried about her because she knows there are lots of problems in Holland at the moment.[186]

*

Her next letter, at the beginning of May 1940 begins by telling Ilse that her last letter took 13 days to get there. 'How slow!' she says. Ilse must have said 'hope to see you soon' in her letter as Hulda says this made her really excited but comments that Ilse mustn't joke about her trip because if it doesn't work out it would be such a disappointment for her. She tells Ilse not to worry about money as she's sure they'll have enough between them.

Anni also wants to visit Hulda but has written that she hasn't got enough money.

"By the way," writes Hulda, "don't tell Anni that I'm paying for your B&B here as I really can't afford to pay for her too. So keep your mouth shut! I think in the end she will manage to visit me here, probably at the end of summer. If you both visited at the same time I could more easily contribute to her stay. But I'm not letting her know this."

She ends the letter with a description of the countryside that surrounds Nice. It's very kitsch she says as the colours are so unreal that they are normally only found on postcards.

---

[186] Letter dated 18 April 1940 from Hulda Frankenbusch to Ilse Frankenbusch.

"I recently walked over the clover fields and it was a dream! Everything is in blossom and, you know, roses and clover flower two or three times here throughout the whole summer!"

Unfortunately the weather has been awful recently with almost non-stop rain and quite cold. Hulda thinks she has inherited Gisela's rheumatic legs because when it rains she gets painful legs and can hardly move.

"That was not a nice time," she says, "but today it's a lot better."

She ends the letter by sending Ilse lots of kisses.

"Am I allowed to say 'see you soon'?" she asks, "I don't dare! Dear, dear God, let it be true!"[187]

---

[187]  Letter dated 3 May 1940 from Hulda Frankenbusch to Ilse Frankenbusch.

# Chapter 7

## 1940
### May
### to
### December

The Norwegian invasion was the precursor to the invasions of Belgium, Holland and France that were to follow.

On 10 May 1940, in a sudden move that took everyone by surprise, the Germans attacked from the west. On 15 May, the Dutch surrendered and on the 18th Belgium followed.

On the 14 May 1940 during the attack on Rotterdam two out of the four Heniger menswear shops were destroyed together with all the stock.[188] Luckily there was no loss of life but it was a drastic blow for the family that Anni had married into. A photo taken before the bombing shows a three storey building with a double-fronted shop on the ground floor. There is one small display window and one large one with the entrance door between them. Both windows are displaying men's headwear – flat caps, bowler hats and trilbies. A striped awning – not in use on the day the photo was taken – shows above the window and the name *Piet Heniger* is printed on the windows and on a sign above the door. A date on the photo indicates that the business was in existence from 1895 until the 14 May 1940. A second photo shows a four storey building with a small shop on the ground floor, this one with a single window and double doors next to it. The name above the frontage is *W.F. Lichtenauer* (the Lichtenauers were part of the extended Heniger family) and on the back of the photo is written 'W.F. Lichtenauer before 14 May 1940'.

*Rotterdam after the German bombing*

---

[188] Letter dated 15 Feb 2009 from Vera Heniger to Sonia Waterfall.

This unexpected move by the Germans brought to an end any travel plans that Ilse and Anni might have been making to go and stay with their mother and the tone of the next letter from Hulda has changed completely.  She sounds almost hysterical as she worries about what might have happened to Anni and how the invasion of France has changed her own circumstances.

"What can we do to know if she [Anni] survived this terrible time, she and Wim," she says, "Did they get away in time?" [189]

Hulda must have heard that as the Dutch army capitulated, a large number of the country's 140,000 Jews rushed to the North Sea coast in the hope of finding some way to reach England. At the same time, according to various estimates, some 200 Jews committed suicide during the week beginning 15 May 1940.[190] No wonder Hulda was beside herself with worry. In Holland the definition of who was a Jew was essentially the same as outlined in the Nuremberg laws of Germany: a person was considered Jewish if they were descended from three or more grandparents who were Jewish . By this definition, Anni although married to Wim, an Aryan, would still have qualified as a Jew.

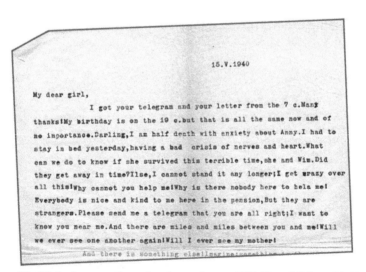

*Hulda's letter after the invasion of Holland May 1940*

[189]  Letter dated 15 May 1940 from Hulda Frankenbusch to Ilse Frankenbusch

[190]  Friedlander, Saul. The years of extermination: Nazi Germany and the Jews 1939-1945. London, Phoenix, 2007. p.121.

During the first months of the occupation, German domination seemed quite mild. The Dutch were considered a kindred race and the Nazi envoys sent to Holland did not foresee any major difficulties in handling the Dutch population and its Jews. Queen Wilhelmina and the government had fled to London but the country continued to be run by an efficient bureaucracy and police force which the Germans took over and supervised. Soon after the defeat, a new political party, the Dutch Union (*Nederlandse Unie*), gained wide support among the population. It also received a certain amount of support from the Germans and it initiated a policy of collaboration similar to the one that the Vichy government in Unoccupied France was to follow. It was in this collaborationist manner that the first anti-Jewish measures were introduced throughout the summer of 1940.[191]

\*

With all the worry about Anni bearing down on her, Hulda asks Ilse to send her a telegram to let her know that she is alright.

"There are miles and miles between you and me!" she says, "Will we ever see one another again! Will I ever see my mother!"

To make matters worse she is having money problems. She hasn't received her allowance from Morgan Bank that week and therefore hasn't been able to pay for her lodgings.

"What will become of me?" she writes, and again at the end of the letter, she repeats "What will become of me?"[192]

\*

On 15 May 1940 Germany turned against France, entering the country through the Ardennes which was totally undefended as the Allies had made the mistake of believing that Flanders would be the main field of battle as it had been in World War I. As a result of this, and also the superior German communications and tactics, the Battle of France was shorter than anyone could have thought. It lasted six weeks including the *Luftwaffe* bombing of Paris on June 3 after which France surrendered on June 22.[193]

---

[191]   Ibid. footnote 190. p. 122.

[192]   Frankenbusch, Hulda. Op. cit. footnote 189.

147

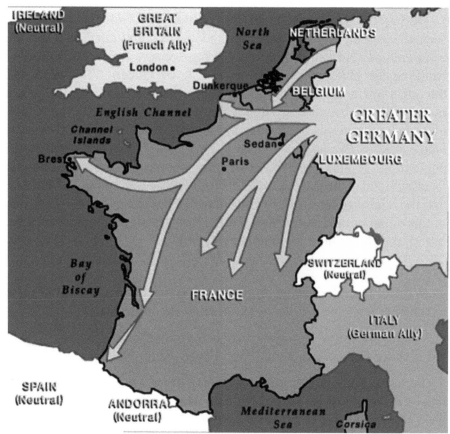

*German invasion of Belgium, Holland and France, 1940.*

Realising that any further defence of France could lead to the annihilation of the British forces, the Commander of the British Expeditionary Force, General Viscount Gort, ordered the retreat back to the port of Dunkirk, an action that would save the British Army to fight another day.[194] For a few weeks, the British population braced itself for invasion, but Hitler hesitated, decided to consolidate his conquests so far and the moment passed. The people of Britain breathed a collective sigh of relief and were then able to concentrate their efforts on making sure that the soldiers on the beaches at Dunkirk

[193]  Wikipedia. War comes to the west.
http://en.wikipedia.org/wiki/European_Theatre_of_World_War_II. Accessed 26 April 2013.

[194]  Eye Witness to History. The evacuation at Dunkirk, 1940.
http://eyewitnesstohistory.com/dunkirk.htm. Accessed 26 April 2013.

were brought home.[195] A call went out for ships to help with the rescue and on 26 May an armada of all kinds of boats – motorboats, sloops, fishing boats, yachts, ferries and barges – made its way across the Channel to rescue the waiting troops. The operation, code-named Dynamo, continued until 4 June 1940 and by the end of it 340,000 British and French soldiers had been evacuated back to England.[196]

During this dreadful month of May 1940 when it seemed that Hitler was going to take over the entire land mass of Europe, there was a spark of hope when, on 10 May, Winston Churchill succeeded Neville Chamberlain as Prime Minister of Great Britain. In his opening speech, he offered the population of Britain only 'blood, toil, tears and sweat.' His policy, he said, was war – war against 'a monstrous tyranny, never surpassed in the dark, lamentable catalogue of human crime.'[197]

*

Meanwhile, by the end of May, Hulda has received a postcard and a telegram from Ilse and she thanks her 'darling girl' for this as it gives her new hope. Her money worries continue because even though Morgan Bank have sent her a cheque she, as a foreigner, is unable to cash it without authorisation which could take some time. Then, that very day, her landlady had told all her lodgers that she will have to close the house on the 15 June. Hulda now has to look for new lodgings but isn't sure whether to stay in Nice or move on. She mentions that a fellow lodger, a Russian lady, is going to Biarritz and has offered to take her there if she is interested. She says she is too tired and heart-sick to make a decision and of course cannot go anywhere without money.

"What a terrible time we are living in," she says.[198]

*

---

195  Friedlander, Saul. Op.cit. footnote 190, p.66.

196  Eye Witness to History. Op.cit. footnote 194.

197  Baker, Nicholson. Human smoke; the beginnings of World War II, the end of civilization. London, Simon & Schuster, 2008, p. 176.

198  Postcard dated 30 May 1940 from Hulda Frankenbusch to Ilse Frankenbusch.

Five days later Ilse receives a postcard with Hulda's new address – Pension Les Charmettes, 6 Rue Francois Aune, Nice. Hulda tells her that she had to sell her type-writer and her golden hat pin. She didn't feel she had any choice as the other lodging closed and she had to pay her debts. Now she is rather sad and worn out with the move and will stay in bed for the rest of the day.[199]

The next letter is more positive as she has received a letter from Ilse with 10 shillings in it which has cheered her up. The same day she has had a letter from Morgan Bank, enclosing, in cash, her allowance for June.

"So," she says, "the worst is over."

She still hasn't managed to get her cheque cashed but has been to the Consulate and they have been trying to help. However, although the staff there have been very kind and helpful, there's not much they can do because it is a new law.

"And what will happen next month nobody knows," she ends.[200]

*

The next postcard a week later is from Biarritz. She says she has just arrived and is exhausted and after posting the card with her new address – 6, *Rue du Port Vieux*, Biarritz – she will go to sleep. She is again worried about money and says 'after the news of the last few days' she doesn't know if her July allowance from Paris will reach her.[201]

The 'news of the last few days' would have been the news of Italy entering the war on the side of Germany and the occupation of part of France by Nazi Germany.Three fifths of the country had been occupied by the German army by mid-June 1940. A new French regime centred in the resort town of Vichy, administered unoccupied France under the terms of an armistice negotiated with the victorious Germans.

---

[199]  Postcard dated 5 June 1940 from Hulda Frankenbusch to Ilse Frankenbusch.

[200]  Postcard dated 9 June 1940 from Hulda Frankenbusch to Ilse Frankenbusch.

[201]  Postcard dated 15 June 1940 from Hulda Frankenbusch to Ilse Frankenbusch.

*Postcard from Biarritz, June 1940.*

The Vichy regime, reacting against the Third Republic whose legitimacy had vanished with the defeat of the French army, launched unoccupied France on the programme they called the National Revolution: authoritarian, traditionalist, pious and neutral in the war between Hitler and the Allies. Vichy was also publicly and conspicuously anti-Semitic and set about solving what it saw as a 'Jewish problem' in France.[202]

*

Biarritz, on the far southwest coast of France now became part of the Occupied Zone as did the entire coastline of the country. However, it probably took a few months for things to change in that part of the country being, as it was, a long way from the seat of power in Paris.

Certainly nothing much seems to have changed for Hulda – a week later she is still in Biarritz, her luggage has arrived and a letter from Ilse, including Frs 353, has been forwarded from Nice. She says she is alright for the time being but that life in Biarritz is not 'very agreeable ... very expensive and rather sad!'

"What will come next?" she asks. "All this tragedy around me is awful! And what shall become of all of us?"

Suddenly her idyllic corner of France has become surrounded by enemies and she must have been feeling trapped.[203]

Meanwhile, in England on 10 June 1940, the government had ordered the detention of all enemy aliens between the ages of sixteen and seventy. Not to be tortured or beaten, as in Dachau, where many had already been held – just to be deprived of their liberty for several years. Churchill knew that many of the Germans who were being imprisoned were enemies of the Nazis.

"I am very sorry for them," he said, "but we cannot, at the present time, and under the present stress, draw all the distinctions that we would like to."[204]

Ilse's aunt, Irma Lange, and her son Hanns were two of the many German Jews who were interned. Irma was sent to Holloway Prison and Hanns was interned on the Isle of Wight. Ilse somehow escaped internment.

---

[202] Marrus, Michael R & Paxton, Robert O. Vichy France and the Jews. NY, Basic Books, 1981. Introduction xii.

[203] Postcard dated 20 June 1940 from Hulda Frankenbusch to Ilse Frankenbusch.

[204] Baker, Nicholson. Op.cit. footnote 197. p.194.

**Controled by Military Command in Brussels**
LILLE○

**Coastal zone forbidden to French from April 1944**

PARIS ○

**Alsace & Moselle**
STRASBOURG
**Annexed by Germany**

**Occupied by Germany from 1940 - 1944**
○ NANTES

VICHY○

LYON○

BRIANÇON○

**Occupied by Italy Nov 1942 - Sep 1943**

○ BORDEAUX

**Free France until 11th Nov 1942**

NICE○

○ BIARRITZ     ○ TOULOUSE     MARSEILLE

*Divided France, June 1940 - 44*

The postcard of 20 June 1940 was the last existing communication from Hulda for nearly three months and when she next contacts Ilse it is in September by telegram from her previous address in Nice. By this time, the Battle of Britain had begun and the first British air raid on Berlin had taken place. Germany had launched its *Blitzkrieg* on Great Britain and bombed Coventry and Birmingham as well as London. On 7 September 1940 the Blitz on London begins in earnest – the first of 57 consecutive nights of strategic bombing, finally ending at the end of October.[205] The war is escalating rapidly.

\*

---

[205]   Wikipedia. 1940 in the United Kingdom.
http://en.wikipedia.org/wiki/1940_in_the_United_Kingdom. Accessed 26 April 2013.

From now on there are fewer letters and more telegrams between Hulda and Ilse, the telegrams sometimes only amounting to a single sentence, obviously just to keep in touch and reassure each other that they are both still alive, in good health and thinking of each other. The first one consisted only of their two addresses so this could be the one Hulda sent to let Ilse know that she was back in Nice. At that time Ilse was living at Yateley House, Godstone Road, Kenley, Surrey and Hulda at *Pension Charmettes, 6 Rue Francois Aune*, Nice. The next telegram, almost a month later was sent to Ilse at 4 Selcroft Road, Purley, Surrey and Hulda says she is happy to have received Ilse's last telegram, that she is content and healthy, as are Grandmother, Anni, Walter and Robert. She sends her kisses.[206] 4 Selcroft Road was the house that Irma and Hanns lived in for over 60 years until Hanns' death in 2007 so it seems likely that Ilse moved in there to take care of the house during the period that her aunt and cousin were interned.

*

Early the following month, Hulda's next telegram says almost the same but adds that she is always very anxious.[207] It is no wonder that she is anxious because by this time Japan has signed a treaty with Germany and Italy, thus forming the Berlin-Rome-Tokyo alliance and turning what had started as a European war into a global one.

On the 12 November 1940 Hulda sends Ilse best wishes, love and kisses for her 25th birthday [on 9 November] from herself, Anni and Wim.[208]

*

At the end of November, Ilse receives one of very few existing letters from her fiancé, Roman, in Vienna:

It is a letter full of sadness, love and longing and asks Ilse to have faith in their future together and not lose hope. He says that he still sees them as having a life together sometime.

---

[206]  Telegram dated 7 October1940 from Hulda Frankenbusch to Ilse Frankenbusch.

[207]  Telegram dated 31 October 1940 from Hulda Frankenbusch to Ilse Frankenbusch.

[208]  Telegram dated 12 November 1940 from Hulda Frankenbusch to Ilse Frankenbusch.

"Don't forget our beautiful Christmas tree in 1938." He writes at the end, "Don't forget your Roman."[209]

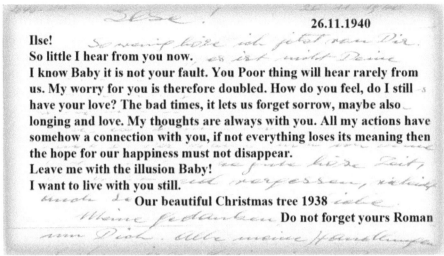

**Ilse!**
So little I hear from you now.
I know Baby it is not your fault. You Poor thing will hear rarely from us. My worry for you is therefore doubled. How do you feel, do I still have your love? The bad times, it lets us forget sorrow, maybe also longing and love. My thoughts are always with you. All my actions have somehow a connection with you, if not everything loses its meaning then the hope for our happiness must not disappear.
Leave me with the illusion Baby!
I want to live with you still.
Our beautiful Christmas tree 1938
Do not forget yours Roman

*Roman's letter to Ilse November 1940*

Allowing what might have got lost in the translation, it sounds as if Roman was almost accepting that Ilse might be moving away from him emotionally. Communication between London and Vienna was always very uncertain and usually letters had to pass through the hands of a third person in a neutral country first. Many got lost in transition so it is really not surprising that their relationship was suffering.

\*

At the end of the year Hulda received a letter from Morgan Bank which must have solved all her money worries in one fell swoop and brought a sense of relief to what had been a difficult year. It tells her that they are transferring the sum of Frs 3,000 from the account of 'Madame la Princesse Margaret Boncompagni', following a cable they have received from New York.[210]

The last communication from Hulda to Ilse in 1940 was a telegram just before Christmas, wishing her all the best for the festive season and sending her a million kisses.[211]

\*

---

[209]   Letter dated 26 November1940 from Roman Rost to Ilse Frankenbusch.

[210]   Letter dated 14 December 1940 from Morgan Bank to Hulda Frankenbusch.

In Britain during November and December, the Blitz continued, spreading outward from London to include Coventry, Birmingham, Southampton, Bristol, Sheffield, Liverpool and Manchester, all strategically important industrial or naval targets from the German point of view. Hitler's plans for invasion included air superiority as an essential factor. As well as the cities they targeted, the *Luftwaffe* concentrated on the destruction of the Royal Air Force both on the ground and in the air. Hitler never gained the air superiority he needed and by the end of the year his plans for invasion had been suspended. Churchill famously said of the R.A.F. personnel who fought in the battle:

"Never in the field of human conflict has so much been owed by so many to so few."[212]

*

1940 had been a year of hope and desperation for the three women. Hope for Hulda as she left Paris and arrived in Nice to a more relaxed lifestyle. For a couple of months the war seemed a long way away. Desperation, as she feared for Anni's life when Holland fell to the Nazis and as she feared she might never see her daughters or mother again.

Ilse was losing hope as she and Roman drifted slowly apart because of communication difficulties as Hitler threatened to take over the whole of Europe. Living on the outskirts of London as she was, she must also have been affected by the Blitz although there is no mention of this in Hulda's letters.

For Gisela in Vienna, hope was fading fast as she became more and more isolated and lived in fear inside her apartment. Like many of the remaining Jews in Vienna, she hardly dared leave the building. It was becoming increasingly common for people to be picked up on the streets on the most insignificant pretexts and to be placed into one of the transports that were leaving Vienna more and more frequently.

---

[211] Telegram dated 22 December 1940 from Hulda Frankenbusch to Ilse Frankenbusch.

[212] Wikipedia. Op.cit. footnote 193.

For all three of them, the letters between them were becoming increasingly important and offered a moment of hope in an ever darkening world.

There would be little in the way of a festive season for the three women and all of them would be relieved that 1940 was over and wonder what 1941 had in store for them and whether it could be any worse than the year gone by.

# Chapter 8

## 1941

Life in Vienna was becoming increasingly difficult for the remaining Austrian Jews as Hitler's plans to get rid of the Jewish population in the Greater German Reich continued to be implemented. Since the *Anschluss*, the Nazi leadership in the city had repeatedly attempted to confiscate as much Jewish-owned property as possible, either by systematically forcing the inhabitants to move into other Jewish houses or, as was proposed in October 1940, by having most of the 60,000 elderly and impoverished Jews still living in the city, deported.

Three months later in January 1941, Hitler approved the deportation of the 60,000 Jews still living in Vienna into the General Government region of Poland and informed the General Governor in Krakow of his decision. The deportations started at the beginning of February and within two months around 7,000 Viennese Jews were shipped off to Poland, mainly to a camp in the Lublin district and a ghetto in Kielce. [213]

On 19 Feb 1941 *The New York Times* said. "Most of them are very old or very young."[214]

Goebbels heard about the recent deportations.

"Vienna will soon be entirely Jew-free," he noted in his diary. It was March 18 1941.[215]

However by then, the increasing military traffic relating to the build up for the invasion of the Soviet Union put an end to these deportations for the time being.[216]

*

The first communication of 1941 was a message sent via the Red Cross in January from Roman to Ilse using Gisela's address in Vienna. He tells Ilse that her grandmother is healthy as are also Hansi's parents. He thinks of Ilse always, his love for her is without end and he will wait for her.[217] Hulda also sent her a telegram the same month

---

[213] Friedlander, Saul. The years of extermination: Nazi Germany and the Jews 1939-1945. London, Phoenix, 2008, p. 138.
[214] Baker, Nicholson. Human smoke: the beginnings of World War II, the end of civilization. London, Simon & Schuster, 2008. p.288.
[215] Ibid. footnote 214, p.297.
[216] Friedlander, Saul. Op.cit. footnote 213, p.139.
[217] Telegram dated 11 January 1941 from Roman Rost to Ilse Frankenbusch.

saying how happy she was to have received Ilse's last letter and that Granny and Roman send kisses.[218]

At the beginning of February, Ilse receives a brief letter from Gisela saying how little she hears from both Hulda and Ilse and how much she hopes that both are healthy and that everything is alright with them. She says that Roman visits her a couple of times a week and that all they talk about is the two of them.

"He is unchanged," she says, "dear and good."

There is not much news to tell – all they can do is wait. She is thankful that she is healthy so far.

"But," she says, "one does not get any younger." [she is now aged 71]

She has heard from Anni – they are doing well and have opened a new shop but Wim's father died four weeks ago. She asks if Ilse has heard from her father, or from Hansi or Rudi and signs off by telling Ilse to continue being brave and sends her a thousand kisses.[219]

Ilse writes back immediately saying she is 'so happy to receive news after such a long time' and that she is glad to hear that Gisela is well.

"You are a brave grandmother!" she says.

She passes on news from friends and relatives they both know – she has visited Aunty Szerena and Alice and also Mr and Mrs Bauer. Aunty Irma is well and sees Hanns, who lives nearby, every three weeks. Father is still in Birmingham but has no work. She has recently had a letter from Anni and gets a telegram from Hulda every three weeks. Hansi is working as a maid and lives near her sister Greta who has recently had an operation for cancer and isn't expected to live much longer. She asks her grandmother for news of friends and relatives in Austria.

"Who is still alive and who is dead?" she asks.

She mentions her friend Christel and asks whether Gisela or Roman can find out what she is up to.

---

[218]    Telegram dated 21 January 1941 from Hulda Frankenbusch to Ilse
        Frankenbusch.
[219]    Letter from Gisela Kerber to Ilse Frankenbusch, undated.

"I miss home so much!" she says at the end of the letter, "Sometimes I think I should never have gone away! It is easier to be poor at home than it is in a foreign country! Grandmother you must be brave and stick things out so that we can all be happy! Stay well old one and look after yourself and thank Roman from me for being so nice to you. It is good for me to know that he is looking after you."[220]

*

After months with the only communication between them being telegrams, Hulda writes in February saying that she has heard that letters to England are reaching their destination so she is hoping her letter gets through. She has been longing to write to Ilse and telegrams are so unsatisfactory and also expensive.

*Letter from Hulda to Ilse, February 1941.*

---

[220] Letter dated 12 February 1941 from Ilse Frankenbusch to Gisela Kerber.

Her allowance from the Princess didn't arrive in July or August, nor in November or January and this month she only got Frs 2000 – much less than before. She is trying to contact the Princess and asks Ilse to try as well. She wants to know all about Ilse's life. What kind of job does she have? Does she earn enough? Where are Irma and Hanns? Hulda says that she has had word from Jeno Kun in Budapest who has had a letter from his daughter Alice in January and she mentioned that Ilse was alright.

She has heard nothing at all from Anni and very little from Grandma. She says that Gisela always mentions Roman, how good he is to her and that his mother always sends her nice things to eat. He seems to be very sad and anxious about Ilse. They have both sent letters to Ilse via Lisbon and Hulda asks if Ilse's father, Rudolf, is really in Lisbon.

She describes her life in Nice and says "life here is, if not easy, at least bearable."

"I am getting thin," she says, "like nearly everybody, 53kg with my winter coat on."

Her heart is weak and will continue like that into the future and there is not much she can do about it.

"But," she says, "I am willing to get through by all means, because I want to live to be together with you all – with Grandma, with Anni and Wim and, above all, with you."

She reminds Ilse that they have been apart now for more than two years.

She ends by saying that Robert is now her most regular correspondent – he is in Morocco, working hard but always full of hope and good humour and letters seem to reach him regularly both from France and from his wife in England. She suggests that Ilse could try writing letters to her via Robert and gives his addres: Robert Miskolczy, No.91075, Group A Aravaill. etrang ¼ Section, Bou-Arfa, Maroc.[221]

*

---

[221] Letter dated 12 February 1941 from Hulda Frankenbusch to Ilse Frankenbusch.

From Ilse's letter it sounds as if this is also the first time for a few months that she has tried to get a letter through to Hulda and she asks her mother to reply via a Portuguese address – c/o PO Box 506, Lisbon, Portugal. She tells her that Hanns and Irma are away and this was probably the period during which they were interned. Ilse is looking after their house and has let out two of the rooms. She has worked as a daily maid and then as a housekeeper for two months and that was the best job she has had since she arrived.

Next week she is going to be a waitress and thinks she will enjoy that too. She will be working in the same building as Mr Bauer – such good luck! She has to work hard but makes enough to earn a living so can't complain. Life is very expensive and she can no longer afford to go to the pictures or theatre, but she is a member of the largest library in town and is reading a lot of very good books.

"The worst thing," she says, "is to live without love."

All the people around 'are very nice but they are strangers' and sometimes she can't bear to look when the mother who is living in the house with her, kisses her daughter.

"I hope, darling," she says at the end of her letter, "that you are alright and have enough money to live on! Please take good care of yourself and keep your chin up! These stressful times must come to an end soon and then we will be happy again, and will always stay together! And then I will look after you and make your life as happy as possible."[222]

*

Hulda replies a month later.

"Yes darling," she writes, "then we will stay together and try to build up a new life for us! If there would not be this hope for the future, I really would not have the strength to go through these hard times."

She describes her lodging as a very cheap *pension* with ugly rooms and rather bad meals but says that spring in Nice is beautiful with everything already in bloom. However it would mean so much more to her if Ilse was there to share the splendour with her. Her greatest pleasure at the moment comes from the letters she receives from Ilse,

---

[222] Letter dated 10 February 1941 from Ilse Frankenbusch to Hulda Frankenbusch.

Anni and Grandma. She tells Ilse that she is lucky to be working close to Mr Bauer and says she wishes she had someone who would show her some kindness and whom she could trust. She comments on the rather tense atmosphere around her at the moment.

"Here," she says, "everybody looks at you with cold and hostile eyes. Everything has changed so much around here! This is not the same country and not the same people I liked so much! They are unhappy and they are poor and hungry and that makes them cruel and unjust. I am sure that when this is all over, they will go back to their old nature, but at the moment it is rather stressful to live with them."

"You can never tell," she continues, "what the next day will bring. We refugees always live in a state of anxious waiting - each morning is full of fear for the coming day!"

As usual, she is having money problems and her allowance from the Princess is only arriving once every six weeks – sometimes even eight weeks. She asks Ilse to write a 'rather imploring letter' to the Princess and gives her the address: Princess Margaret Boncompagni, Hotel Mayflower, Washington, Massachusetts.[223]

*

Meanwhile, in Holland, the registration of Dutch Jews with the German authorities had begun in January. Deportations were to begin the following month and on 22 February hundreds of Jewish men were arrested on the streets of Amsterdam. On the 25 February tens of thousands of Dutch citizens participated in a general strike to protest the deportation of Jews from their country – the only such strike in Europe. Amsterdam was paralysed and soon the strike spread to other cities. The Germans reacted with extreme violence and many Dutch citizens were killed or wounded and the demonstrators arrested. The strike was quashed and the Dutch learned that the Germans would not hesitate to pursue their anti-Jewish policies with extreme ruthlessness. Those arrested were deported in June, first to Buchenwald and then to Matthausen where all 348 perished by suicide, shooting, beating or other forms of torture.[224]

Surrounded by such events, Anni, in an undated letter written in the spring of that year, announces to Hulda that she is pregnant and the

---

[223]   Letter dated 15 March 1941 from Hulda Frankenbusch to Ilse Frankenbusch.
[224]   Friedlander, Saul. Op.cit. footnote 213, p.178.

baby is due in September. In a letter to Ilse, Hulda says that it's a bit of a joke thinking of herself as a grandma, but that she is happy for Anni and Wim. She mentions how much she would like to be with Anni in the coming months.

"I'd like to be able to take care of her," she says, "and make everything as easy as possible for her!"[225]

*

A letter from Gisela to Hulda indicates that she has heard about Anni's pregnancy and wants to knit something for the baby but will wait a while until she hears that Anni is well. She tells Hulda not to worry that she hasn't heard from Anni as they both know she is not a writer of letters.

The day before she had gone to the Jewish cemetery in Vienna to spend time with her husband who was buried there. She prayed for them all. She is sad that Hulda is having sleepless nights and not able to eat properly because she is worried about her mother and tells her to remain healthy and believe that there has to be a reunion in the future.[226]

*

Back in Nice, Hulda sends Ilse a backup telegram in case her letter didn't get through, repeating the news about Anni and saying that she is in good health but without money. She has received the letter sent via Lisbon but has heard nothing from Ilse's friends. She has had a letter from Grandma and Roman sends kisses.[227] Another telegram six weeks later says that she has had a letter from Roman and she passes on his messages of love for Ilse. He says that he always thinks of her and hopes for their future happiness. At the end of May a further telegram to Ilse thanks her for her birthday wishes [Hulda was 51 on 19 May 1941] and says she is healthy but very lonely.

---

[225] Letter dated 15 March 1941 from Hulda Frankenbusch to Ilse Frankenbusch.
[226] Letter dated 7 April 1941 from Gisela Kerber to Hulda Frankenbusch.
[227] Telegram dated 21 March 1941 from Hulda Frankenbusch to Ilse Frankenbusch.

*Telegram announcing Anni's pregnancy, March 1941*

*

In Holland in April 1941 a Central Office for Jewish Emigration was established in Amsterdam, on the same model as the offices set up first in Vienna and later in Berlin and Prague in 1939. Such offices took over the registration of the Jewish population, its property and its departure from the country (including the confiscation of any abandoned property). The intention was for it to control all significant aspects of Jewish affairs in Holland. In August 1941 the Jews of Holland were ordered to register all their assets and in September real estate was included in the registration.[228]

Meanwhile, Anni had miscarried her baby after five months, the miscarriage being caused by an excess of amniotic fluid.[229] Hulda's hopes of becoming a grandmother were dashed and she worried continuously about Anni and agonised over the distance between herself, her daughters and her mother.

*

Back in France in June 1941 a new legislative package had been introduced, which, amongst other elements, included a detailed census of all Jews in the Unoccupied Zone. This move was to have fatal

---

[228]   Friedlander, Saul. Op.cit. footnote 213, p.179.
[229]   Letter dated 30 July 2009 from Vera Heniger to Sonia Waterfall.

consequences later when Jews were being rounded up and deported. Before the 31 July 1941 all Jews had to make an elaborate declaration in person. They were asked about children, parents, grandparents, religious affiliation, education, military service and professional activity as well as property, income, debts etc.

A further element of the law introduced in June was the extension of the 'Aryanization' of Jewish business and property to the Unoccupied Zone. The census had already provided the government with detailed information about Jewish property, this law empowered the state to confiscate it. The number of Jewish businesses in the south of the country had increased substantially, when, in an attempt to escape Aryanization in the north, financial resources had been moved across the border between the two zones.[230]

*

At the same time as these events occurred in France, Operation Barbarossa, the code-name for the Nazi invasion of the Soviet Union had begun when German tanks crossed the Meml river into Soviet-controlled Lithuania. It was 22 June 1941.[231]

As recently as ten days earlier Stalin had informed his generals "Germany is busy with the war in the west and I am certain that Hitler will not yet risk creating a second front by attacking the Soviet Union. Hitler is not such an idiot."[232]

*

Also in June, Ilse received a letter from the Red Cross – from Mary Campion O.B.E, an Assistant Deputy Director of the International Relations Department who would figure largely in Ilse's life for the next two years or more. It appears that Ilse had followed up on Hulda's request that she try and contact Princess Margaret Boncompagni as this letter outlines a reply received from the American Red Cross in Washington who had managed, in turn, to contact the Princess. The Princess has confirmed that Hulda was her secretary-housekeeper during her stay in Fiume from 1922 to 1924 and says that if Hulda wanted to move to England to join Ilse then the Princess would be

---

[230] Marrus, Michael R & Paxton, Robert O. Vichy France and the Jews. NY, Basic Books, 1981, ps.100 – 101.
[231] Baker, Nicholson. Op.cit. footnote 214, p.344.
[232] Baker, Nicholson. Op.cit. footnote 214, p.340.

'very glad to facilitate it.' The Princess doesn't think there is any possibility of Hulda moving to America under war conditions but is willing to continue sending her the US$70 per month through Morgan Bank that she has been sending up to now. If Hulda were to move to England this arrangement would be continued through Morgan & Co in London. The American Red Cross suggest that Hulda should contact the Princess directly or through them in which case they would forward the letters on.[233]

Mary Campion then writes to Ilse a week later to suggest that they should have a meeting to talk over the matter of Hulda's circumstances.[234]

*

A telegram from Hulda says that she is happy to have heard from Ilse the good news that she is content and in good health. There is no news from *Oma* [Gisela] or Anni. [235]

A letter to Ilse from a J.Martin of the Aliens Department of the Home Office must have made her despair of ever seeing her mother again.

"In the present circumstances," Mr Martin writes, "it is regretted that facilities for the entry into the United Kingdom for your mother, Mrs Hulda Frankenbusch cannot be granted."[236]

This sounds such a final decision that the news must have been devastating for both Hulda and Ilse.

---

[233] Letter dated 20 June 1941 from Mary Campion to Ilse Frankenbusch.
[234] Letter dated 30 June 1941 from Mary Campion to Ilse Frankenbusch.
[235] Telegram dated 8 July 1941 from Hulda Frankenbusch to Ilse Frankenbusch.
[236] Letter dated 18 July 1941 from J. Martin from the Home Office (Aliens Department) to Ilse Frankenbusch.

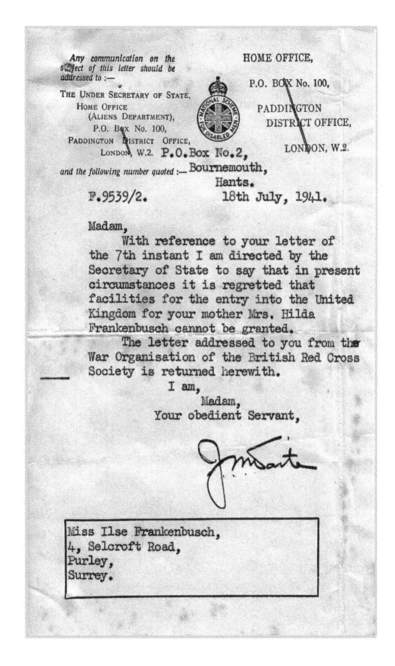

Letter from the Home Office, July 1941

After this there is no further communication between the three women for three months.

*

Meanwhile, in July, Rudolf Hoss had been ordered to prepare an extermination camp at Auschwitz in Poland – he was to be the commandant there until late 1943. The following month the first 4300 Jews are sent from Paris to Drancy, a camp on the outskirts of the city. These are the first of 70,000 Jews in France who will be deported to Drancy and from there to extermination camps further east including Auschwitz.[237]

*

A telegram from Hulda at the end of October thanks Ilse for her news about *Oma*, Anni and Roman. Hulda herself is in good health but very lonely and sad and worried and fearful about Ilse. The last telegram to Ilse in 1941 comes a month later when Hulda reassures Ilse that she didn't forget her birthday but her money had only just arrived today.[238]

*

Dear Anita!
Why no sign of life? I am very worried. Have also no news from Mum and Ilse. I feel terribly lonely – because I have no one here anymore. My Cousin Aunt Schäfer has poisoned herself three weeks ago – out of fear for the future and so one hears and sees only sad things. Please dear Annele write to me how you All are. Do you have any news? From fatherl, from Hanne? Be hugged and kissed, from Vienna to Ma Heniger Willy and Family.
Yours Grossmuttl

*Gisela's last letter, December 1941*

---

237  Baker, Nicholson. Op.cit. footnote 214, p.360.
238  Telegram dated 21 November 1941 from Hulda Frankenbusch to Ilse Frankenbusch.

A final poignant letter in 1941 is from Gisela in Vienna to Anni in Holland and says she has had no news from her or from Ilse or Hulda. She is feeling terribly lonely because there is no-one with her in Vienna any longer. Aunt Schafer poisoned herself three weeks ago out of fear for the future and so Gisela feels surrounded by sadness and fear.[239]

Aunt Julie Schafer was one of thousands of Jews, who, finding life under the Nazis not worth living, committed suicide.

A drug called Veronal was the poison of choice in many cases. Veronal was a barbiturate used medicinally as a drug to induce sleep but an overdose could kill. The dosage required depended very much on body weight and records exist of strong healthy men taking days to die while the people around them hope that death will come before the Gestapo arrive. Many people collected it over time and hoarded it in phials for months until that final moment when life became intolerable.[240]

*

By the end of 1941, Japan had bombed Pearl Harbour on 7 December 1941 and on 8 December the US had declared war on Japan, thus entering World War II. On the same day Japanese troops had landed in the Philippines, French Indochina and British Singapore, thus effectively beginning the war for the Pacific.

On 11 December 1941, Germany and its Axis partners declared war on the US.

Meanwhile, a Soviet counter offensive had driven the Germans from the Moscow suburbs and into a chaotic retreat in the middle of a harsh winter.[241]

The global conflict was now in full swing but the entry of the US into the war would eventually tip the scales on the side of the Allies.

---

[239] Letter dated 10 December 1941 from Gisela Kerber to Anni Heniger.
[240] Veit, Suse, formerly Meyer, Suse. Unpublished account of her wartime experiences, now included in the archive of Jewish wartime experiences in the Wiener Library.
[241] Wikipedia. Timeline of World War II (1941).
http://en.wikipedia.org/wiki/Timeline_of_World_War_II_(1941). Accessed 19 May 2013.

# Chapter 9

## 1942
### January
### to
### November

In January 1942 the Nazi government held a conference at *Wannsee* in the suburbs of Berlin where the nuts and bolts of a new policy were discussed. The end result was to be the elimination of all Jews from Europe. They were to be transported to camps in Poland where the fittest would be put to work until they died from exhaustion, the unfit would be killed immediately they arrived and any who survived would be murdered as they would represent the strongest of the Jewish population and might one day produce children who would take their revenge. Thus, Hitler's Final Solution came into being as an official policy.

Up until this time Jews had been killed in relatively small numbers and many had been moved into ghettos to keep the Jewish population contained and under control. However the ghettos were becoming seriously overcrowded and as the Nazis took over more and more territory, a solution was needed for the number of Jews now being dealt with. The solution was the extermination camps that had been set up during 1941 and now started being used in earnest. They were at Chelmno, Sobidor, Belzec, Treblinka and Majdanek. The sixth was Auschwitz-Birkenau which was a huge work camp producing goods for the Nazi war effort as well as an extermination camp. It contained barracks, factories, medical centres, huts, gas chambers and crematoria.[242]

Once the death camps were in place then all that was needed was to coordinate rolling stock, timetables, deportation schedules and holding camps. Adolf Eichmann was in charge and his representatives were sent to be attached to German Embassies throughout the conquered nations. They received their instructions from Eichmann's section in Berlin and reported back to him, by telegram, as each deportation was planned and carried out.[243]

\*

Of course, our three women were in ignorance of this meeting and the influence it would have on their lives.

---

[242] Roseman, Mark. The villa, the lake, the meeting: Wannsee and the final solution. London, Penguin Press, 2002.
[243] Gilbert, Martin. The Holocaust. Holt, Rinehart & Winston, 1985, p.284.

For Ilse in London, 1942 proved to be a year of huge changes. In many ways it was the moment in her life when she grew up, started making decisions for herself and started looking to the future. Until this year she had been very involved with her old life in Vienna, still engaged to Roman despite the communication difficulties putting great pressure on the relationship, still dependent on her mother and Gisela and the letters and telegrams that flowed between them and still wishing to return to the three-woman household that was her life in Vienna until 1938. As long as Gisela and Roman were in Vienna, that was where home was.

The early part of the year was one of huge upheavals, the first being when Hulda heard that Roman had married someone else. At the end of January a telegram from Hulda tells Ilse that she has had a letter from *Oma* dated early December the year before and Gisela tells her that is well but Roman has got married. Hulda tells Ilse 'don't be sorry, laugh.'[244] A week later comes another telegram – Hulda is obviously anxiously waiting to hear how Ilse had reacted to the news. "Hope you are well," she says, "courageous and proud."[245]

*

Ilse doesn't respond for another month. In the meantime ordinary life goes on despite heart-breaking news. In early March Ilse receives a letter from the Czechoslovakian Legation in London with her new passport, the news that the consular fee of eight shillings and sixpence has been received and the return of her documents. She is reminded to sign it in her own hand on page three.[246] At last she had got rid of her German passport, was no longer classed as a German citizen and was officially Czechoslovakian again.

---

[244] Telegram dated 27 January 1942 from Hulda Frankenbusch to Ilse Frankenbusch.
[245] Telegram dated 3 February 1942 from Hulda Frankenbusch to Ilse Frankenbusch.
[246] Letter dated 3 March 1942 from K.Vanek, First Secretary, Czechoslovak Legation, London, to Ilse Frankenbusch.

No.1165/42
JS/HK. 3rd March 1942.


Dear Madam,

Replying to your letter of the
26th ultimo, I beg to send you herewith
your new Czechoslovak passport which please
sign in own hand on page 3.
The consular fee of 8s.6d. has
been duly received by this office.
At the same time I beg to return
your documents, namely:Osvědčeni o čs.stát-
ním občanství č.7822/lail938 odd.1., Geburts-
und Tauf-Schein No.1719/30 and Amtsbestati-
gung No.I-2-100.

Yours faithfully,

X.VANĚK,
4 encls. First Secretary.


Miss Ilse Frankenbuschová,
4, Selcroft Road,
Purley, Surrey.

*Letter to Ilse from the Czechoslovakian Legation March 1942.*

*

The second upheaval at the beginning of the year was when Hulda
told Ilse of her grandmother's 'disappearance' in a letter written mid-
March. Hulda mentions a previous message she sent about Gisela's
illness. This time she has even more devastating news.

179

"*Oma,* only half recovered," Hulda writes, "had to leave Vienna for Poland, like so many others."

She hasn't been able to find out when this happened or exactly where she was sent and is sick with fear and desperation. She immediately wrote to the Red Cross in Geneva to see if she could get any information through them. She also tells Ilse that two of her aunts had died, one of them committing suicide, and that Gisela buried them both and had to wind up their affairs. Gisela must have felt so alone after that and then to fall sick and be deported.

"It's unfathomable," Hulda says.[247]

*

It was in Riga, Latvia, that Gisela's life came to an end. It was in January 1942 that a concentration camp was established in Riga providing alternative accommodation to the ghetto which was already in existence. It was a couple of months later that her family discovered that she had been deported and several years later that they discovered where she had been sent. Later in 1942 the International Red Cross reported that their search for Gisela had been inconclusive and they couldn't find out what had happened to her. It appears that she fell ill in Vienna and had to go into hospital. It was while she was there that the Nazis cleared the hospital and sent the inmates east in the middle of winter, some to Poland and some to Latvia.

She was aged 72 when she was deported and whether she died as a result of her illness, old age, cold and exhaustion, or was murdered is unknown. There were several deportations of Viennese Jews in January that could have included Gisela, the first was of a thousand deportees on 9 January from Theresienstadt which was often used as the holding camp for Viennese Jews who were then sent east to concentration camps. Two days later, on 11 January, more than 1500 Jews were seized in Vienna and sent by train to Riga.

One of them, Liana Neumann, provided an eye-witness account.

"There was no water. The coaches were sealed and we could not leave them. It was very cold and we chipped off some of the ice from the windows to have water."

Many froze to death on the journey.

---

[247] Letter dated 16 March 1942 from Hulda Frankenbusch to Ilse Frankenbusch.

"On reaching Riga," she continues, "we were received by SS men, who made us run and beat us up ... old people and children were taken away by force and killed."[248]

The fate of most Jews arriving in Riga in early 1942 was to be taken out to Rumbula Forest and shot.[249]

Throughout January, similar deportations of elderly Jews from Vienna to Theresienstadt and from there to Riga continued and Gisela could have been included in any of these.

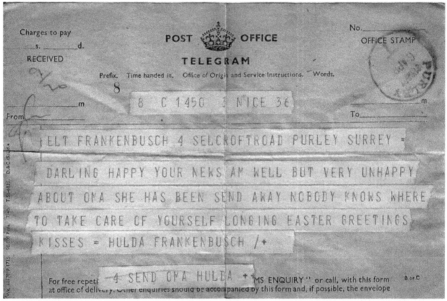

*Hulda's telegram to Ilse about Gisela's deportation, April 1942.*

It was at the end of March that the first deportation of Jews from France to Auschwitz occurred. This was a harbinger of things to come.

\*

In an undated letter, possibly written at the end of March or beginning of April, Ilse at last replies to all the sad news received from Hulda in the first months of the year. She mentions Roman's marriage and says his infidelity was to be expected but that it was still like a

---

[248] Gilbert, Martin. Op.cit. footnote 243, p.250.
[249] United States Holocaust Memorial Museum. Riga.
http://www.ushmm.org/wlc/article.php?lang=en&ModuleId=10005463. Accessed 6 October 2008.

'slap in the face'. The main thing is that she has now lost hope of having a home in the future but says that she still has Hulda and the two of them will make a home together. The news about her grandmother has made her very sad.

"Poor grandmother," she says, "she had such an ugly old age and deserved better."

Despite the bad news she writes that she was so happy to hear from her mother as this letter was the first in a long time.[250]

Roman's marriage, Gisela's deportation and the deaths of other family members broke the last links to Vienna for Ilse. Now there was only Hulda in France and Anni in Holland. From this point onwards it seemed that she made a determined effort to make a life for herself in England.

*

In the same letter that Hulda wrote about Gisela's deportation, she tells Ilse that she is sick with fear and half out of her mind. She tells Ilse that she would not recognise her now – she has gone grey and weighs only 48kg.

"It really is getting too much" she says, "how can one endure?"

She has also had bad news from Paris and all her boxes that had been stored with a shipping agency have been "confiscated – requisitioned or whatever they call it!"

"I lost all my possessions!" She exclaims. "How not to lose your mind!?"

She says she is completely at a loss and feels very "alone and isolated and very, very dispirited". She wants very much to hear from Ilse – everything about her life and work and about the people they both know – Hansi and her sister, Mr Bauer and aunt Szerena and cousin Alice. She hears occasionally from Szerena's husband but he hasn't had any news from his wife and daughter and is also very unhappy.

She mentions that "it is very uncomfortable here" and that she thanks the lord for every day that passes without any serious incidents.

---

[250] Undated letter from Ilse Frankenbusch to Hulda Frankenbusch.

She tells Ilse to take care of herself. She hasn't heard from Anni in months but the money from the Princess arrived on time this month.

"When will this nightmare end and where will it lead to?" she ends the letter, "Where will our destiny lead us before we all meet again? That's my only hope and that hope keeps me going."[251]

*

The Red Cross obviously didn't know that the latest instalment from the Princess arrived on time because Mary Campion wrote to Ilse on the 23 March 1942 to say that she has been having problems finding the address of the Morgan Bank and asks Ilse if she can help as she wants to deal with the whole question of Hulda's money getting to her.[252]

*

Ilse, in the same undated letter from March/April, tells Hulda that she is still a waitress but has had enough of it. The only thing that holds her in the job is the salary. She had 4 weeks off work sick earlier in the year and that ripped a big hole in her savings. She has applied to study at a Dental Hospital but finds it hard to make a decision and wishes Hulda was there to help her. Every time she has to make a decision she tries to think what Hulda would advise her. She tells her mother to look after herself as she needs her urgently and is waiting longingly for the time when they will be together. In the meantime she can only be with Hulda in her thoughts – but "Rest assured that I am, always!"[253]

*

There is an interesting but unsigned letter at the beginning of April from Bagneres de Bigorre, a small place near the French/Spanish border between Bayonne and Perpignan. It is addressed to 'Caporal Miskolzcy' in Bou-Arfa. This would be Robert, a cousin of Hulda's so maybe the letter was forwarded to her to keep her up to date with what was happening to the writer.

---

[251] Frankenbusch, Hulda. Op.cit. footnote 247.
[252] Letter dated 23 March 1942 from Mary Campion, Assistant Deputy Director of the Foreign Relations Department of the British Red Cross Society to Ilse Frankenbusch.
[253] Frankenbusch, Ilse. Op.cit. footnote 250.

Whoever the writer is, he calls Robert 'my good, wonderful old post minister' and in several letters and telegrams between Hulda and Ilse they instruct each other to send replies through Robert. From other letters we discover that he was sent to North Africa to help build the Trans-Saharan Railway and somehow must have been able to provide a safe conduit for letters to and from friends in Europe.

The writer remembers that the last time they met was in Casa at the Pesach Festival in his 'little Moroccan Room.' Since then he has stayed in 'this little corner of Europe' and so far has 'had nothing to complain about.' He spends his time working on his little garden and says that 'nowadays it is necessary due to the lack of food available.'

"You desperately look for people of Jewish origin," he says, "however it is not easy."[254]

*

A month later, in May, Hulda receives Ilse's last letter and replies to it immediately. She answers Ilse's comments about Roman's marriage.

"Why should you not have your own home?" She says, "There are really enough men in the world, even after this world-massacre."

And she tells Ilse to count her blessings.

"You are healthy and working," says Hulda, "and that is more than enough in today's desolate circumstances."

She goes on to give Ilse some idea of what life is like. She says that life in Nice is becoming more expensive and difficult and she lives in a small *pension* in a room in the basement next to the kitchen. It's the cheapest room in the whole house which has twelve rooms in all. She has furnished the room with her own belongings but the house itself is dirty and neglected, like most *pensions* in the South of France. The meals she pays for are only so-so and not very plentiful which is why she only weighs 48kg now. Still, she is reasonably healthy although currently nursing her second bout of bronchial catarrh of the spring, even though it's warm and there's bright sunshine outside.

She says she reads a lot which she should not really do because of her eyes. She no longer goes for long walks because she doesn't want

---

[254] Letter dated 6 April 1942 from an unknown writer to Robert Miskolzcy.

to lose more weight and also because she doesn't feel very strong. Now and then she goes to the cinema or to a good concert but mainly leads an uneventful life.

"Despite life being uneventful," she says, "I thank God for every day that passes uneventfully."

The most beautiful things about Nice are the flowers which are wonderful and give her great joy. If only Ilse was there to enjoy them with her then life would be so different.

"The letter has become longer than expected," says Hulda, "and I feel sorry for the censor who has to read it all."

She ends by saying that Ilse is always in her thoughts and so, always with her.[255]

*

By this time shops in Vichy France are three-quarters empty of merchandise, shoes are being mended with wooden soles, clothes are without any style and dentists are now crowning teeth with steel. People are always hungry after meals and the bars still in business are now used less for drinking and more for meeting, exchanging news, and buying contraband cigarettes.[256]

*

On her birthday Hulda writes to her old friend, Sani Torday, and tells him that his last letter arrived on the eve of her 52nd birthday and that she is writing back to him as a birthday celebration. She reminds him of their 'Birthday bowls' in the *Prater*, the big amusement park in Vienna where the four of them used to go each year on her birthday - Ilse, Roman, Sani and herself. She also tells him about Roman getting married last Christmas but that Ilse is being brave about it. She comments that every day can bring huge changes.

"It's like sitting on a crater that could explode at any minute!" she says, "But I'm preparing myself to hold on because I want to see my girls again."

---

[255] Letter dated 10 May 1942 from Hulda Frankenbusch to Ilse Frankenbusch.
[256] Lambert, Raymond-Raoul. Diary of a witness: 1940-1943. NY, Ivan R. Dee in association with the United States Historical Memorial Museum, 2007, p.108.

"At the moment the financial situation is tolerable" she continues "the princess is caring for me but she is in the USA and that is rather far away and also insecure."

She ends by saying that there are always new things to worry about.[257]

A telegram from Hulda four days later tells Ilse that Robert has had a letter from Sani who was in Amsterdam and has seen Anni. This must have been a great relief at a time when communication was so difficult.

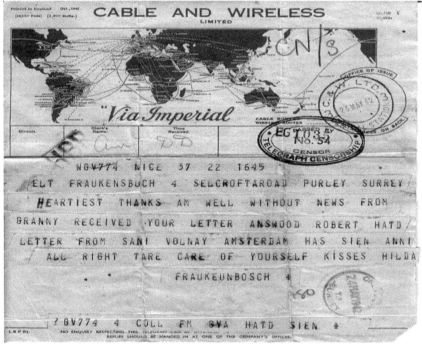

*Telegram from Hulda to Ilse, May 1942.*

\*

Later that month, the Vichy government forbade Jews to access restaurants, cafes, libraries, sportsgrounds, squares and other public places. Whether such a decree could ever be enforced was another matter. It would be interesting to know whether this decree ever affected Hulda or whether she was considered a Protestant which was how she thought of herself.

---

[257] Letter dated 19 May 1942 from Hulda Frankenbusch to Sani Torday.

It was in June 1942 that the Germans imposed on the Jews of the French Occupied Zone the wearing of the star that identified all wearers as Jews. All Jews over the age of six had to wear, on the left side of an outer garment, a star of David the size of the palm of a hand, upon which was written in capital letters the word *Juif* or *Juive*. In the build-up to this decree, the Germans had tried to impose the star on both zones but the Vichy government refused to have anything to do with the matter and it only went ahead in the Occupied Zone. After a few weeks only a third of Jews subject to the decree had actually received stars and maybe it was the recognition of the difficulty of enforcing the law that persuaded the Vichy government to steer well clear of it.[258]

*

June 1942 brought Hulda a most interesting letter from Ilse that must also have been a bit of a shock because for the first time Ilse confessed that she had a 'boyfriend'. She says she only decided to take this step after that painful 'slap' from Roman and then only because this man was so different from Roman. She describes Frank for her mother.

"He is no Adonis", she says, "35 years old and comes from Holland."

She explains that 'he was an officer on a ship that came across, got sick with asthma and now works in a factory.' He is married with three children and his family are all still in Holland. She says that he loves his wife but also wants to see Ilse happy.

"Sexuality is unfortunately an unavoidable evil," says Ilse, "He is the first man with whom I feel entirely balanced and satisfied when he is with me. I know one should not start a relationship with a married man but what good is sensible advice when one does the opposite anyway. At least I know where I stand and understand that at the end of the war he will leave me. I don't expect anything else and I think this is why we get along so well"[259]

She ends this part of the letter saying she hopes that Hulda understands her position because she cares what her mother thinks about such a relationship.

---

[258] Marrus, Michael R & Paxton, Robert O. Vichy France and the Jews. NY, Basic Books, 1981, p.236.
[259] Letter dated 22 June 1942 from Ilse Frankenbusch to Hulda Frankenbusch.

*

Earlier in the letter she had described her working day. She is still waitressing which suits her. She says she could get a more classy job but would only get half the money and would have to feed herself which would be very expensive.

She works for a large company that has hotels, restaurants, coffee houses and buffets everywhere. The building she works in is in the centre of town, occupying almost a whole block and has a coffee house and four restaurants. One is vegetarian and that is where Ilse works.

She continues by describing how she gets up every day at 8am, washes, has breakfast, washes up, dusts and makes her bed. She leaves home at 9.30 each morning to catch the 9.45 train and gets to work at 10.30. From then until 11.45 all the waitresses prepare the tables (each waitress has ten tables), dust, refill the containers etc and then go up to the fifth floor where they change into their uniforms and have a meal.

At 12 o'clock they start to serve and are busy non-stop until 3.45pm. Then they have a 45 minute break and then continue until 7pm when they get changed, have their evening meal and leave work at 7.30 in time for the 7.45 train which gets her home by 8.30pm.

Then, if it's summer, she puts on shorts and works in the garden until 10pm, then has a bath and falls into bed exhausted by 11pm. Her free days are Mondays and every second Sunday when she tidies, washes, irons, shops, writes letters and works in the garden. If the weather is bad she goes to the movies in the evening and her only luxuries are cigarettes and also books, of which she now has a small library.

At the beginning of the letter she had described her life as 'so wonderful that I am ashamed to tell you.' At the time of writing she is on vacation and has taken a private room nearby. She bought herself a bicycle so can now afford to take a holiday because she doesn't need to pay for travel.

"At the moment," she says, "I am lying on my tummy in the grass under a big old tree, am surrounded by rose bushes and the sun is burning my back. In a nutshell, I am at a very nice outdoor pool and feel fantastic!!"

She says she believes she has always been lucky and has landed 'butter side up.'

"I believe I am indestructible," she continues "unless the house gets hit by a bomb."

The whole tone of the letter is positive and it seems that the relationship with Frank has changed her outlook on life and, despite still grieving for her grandmother, she is happy and making the most of her life in London.

"Know that I am so very sad that I cannot ease your burdens," she ends the letter, "Please be my brave mum and stay strong whatever happens!"[260]

*

At the end of July 1942, Robert writes to Ilse. He is obviously acting as a go-between for letters written by Hulda and Ilse.

"It is of course no problem for me to transport your letters to and from each other," he says, "and I am glad that I can be of use."

"I have always been in frequent touch with your mother," he continues, "and still today we are in constant contact. She is always so lovely and manages to get hold of different things for us."

He describes Bou Arfa as 'a godforsaken hole', 130kms from the Sahara. The nearest large towns are 150 kms in any direction.

"The hills are out of stone and there's no vegetation at all so it's just stones and sand," he tells Ilse. "Sandstorms occur daily and there are bugs in the barracks - that's Bou Arfa."[261]

Bou-Arfa was home to the largest Vichy-era labour camp in Morocco. According to the Red Cross 818 people were interned there as of July 1942.[262] Many of them, like Robert, had volunteered for the French Foreign Legion prior to France entering the war and then after the armistice in June 1940 had found themselves treated as prisoners rather than soldiers.

He then tells Ilse what has happened to him since the beginning of the war. At the beginning of the war he went to live in Lagny near

---

[260] Ibid. footnote 259.
[261] Letter dated 26 July 1942 from Robert Miskolczy to Ilse Frankenbusch.
[262] Vichy camps. http://jewishmorocco.org/?page_id=32. Accessed 3 April 2013

Paris and along with many immigrants, he voluntarily signed up to make himself available to the state. He says this is where the adventure began as he was old enough to have already fought in one war and was not very strong.

"But," he says, "I wanted to repay France for being allowed to stay there."

He also hoped that through his service to France, as yet not at war with Germany, he could prevent his wife from being interned. On 29 December 1939 he was called up for the second time in his life and after collecting his belongings from his 'attic room' in Lagny he travelled to a camp in Lyon. Here everyone assembled before travelling for ten days, first to Marseille and then to Sidi Bel Abbes in Algeria.

After three weeks there he was placed in the 2$^{nd}$ Regiment and sent to Meknes in Morocco. He says that it was near Meknes that the youngsters came to do their infantry training, while the older ones, including Robert were sent about 6kms out of town to a '*marabout* camp' [a frontier station – literally, a shrine marking the grave of a Muslim hermit].

Two months later he was transferred to the main barracks in Meknes where he went through a lot of physical training which he coped with well and got a 'good mark.' The 2$^{nd}$ Regiment was supposed to go to Italy but because of the armistice they stayed where they were. As he was one of the eldest there he was given the job of working for a military cooperative, selling coffee, sugar and other food to a thousand people.

He had no chance of being liberated as he didn't have the necessary 10,000 Francs nor relatives in unoccupied territories, so had to stay in Morocco. He was put into a work unit and paid Frs 1.25 per day. The next three months he spent in the 'beautiful' El Hajeb, a health resort with good water, 30 kms from Meknes. At first he was a handyman, carrying stones, weeding the garden etc until a small theatre group was put together and he became a part of that.

"It was a friendly, funny bunch," he says, "and we did good things."

190

At Christmas 1940 just before a big performance he had to leave with the entire work unit for Bou Arfa and this 'god-forsaken nest'. Here his unit was to assist in building a Trans-Saharan railroad for a company called *Mediteranee-Niger.*

"I will never forget our mood as we arrived here," he says, "it literally made us speechless."

They were put together with some Spanish workers who had arrived before them. At first they went on strike and demanded to be moved on but eventually they gave in and started to work. For a month he carried large stones that were to be broken up and used to level the railroad. Then he went to another section and dug the train track. After that he collapsed and was declared incapable but the railroad construction company came to his help and when a job became available in the post office, he was given the job and started work at one of the counters.

He says that this has been OK for him so far. He gets good food, even better than in France and is able to send Hulda 'small food improvements' each month. He signs himself off 'Your old Robert.'[263]

*

Denise Grunewald, *Assistant Sociale* from the *Service Social d'Aide aux Emigrants*, 96 *Rue Garibaldi*, Lyon, sent Ilse a telegram at the end of September saying that Hulda was very anxious, could not cable herself but was alright. She said that an explanation would follow in a letter from Robert and that Ilse herself should only write or cable to Robert.[264]

---

[263] Miskolczy, Robert. Op.cit. footnote 261.
[264] Telegram dated 23 September 1942 from Denise Grunewald to Ilse Frankenbusch.

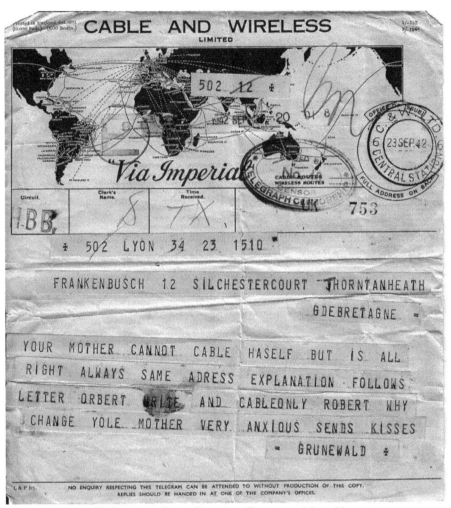

*Telegram from Denise Grunewald to Ilse*
*concerning Hulda, September 1942.*

*

The first of many deportations of 'foreign' Jews from the Unoccupied Zone had taken place. Starting in August regional prefects were directed to deport to the Occupied Zone foreign Jews who had entered France since January 1936. These included all Germans, Austrians, Poles, Czechs, Estonians and refugees from the Soviet Union. The deportees were to be shipped to Drancy, a holding camp on the outskirts of Paris. From there the transports would continue east, sometimes immediately, sometimes after a few days.

The results of the August roundups in the Unoccupied Zone disappointed the Germans and the categories for deportation were widened to include Belgian and Dutch Jews previously exempt. The conditions for exemption – age, family status, military record etc – changed almost daily during September in order to catch more Jews in the police net.

By the beginning of September over 27,000 Jews had been deported from both zones of France and the Germans hoped to add another 25,000 by the end of October. However no convoys left in October, only four in November and then nothing more until the huge roundups and deportations of February 1943 from both zones. The variation in numbers could have been because there weren't enough 'deportables' to be found or, more likely, because there was an unforeseen interruption to the railway timetables.[265]

*

In a letter from the International Migration Service to the British Red Cross, on the last day of September it was mentioned that Hulda had been arrested in August but had managed to persuade the authorities that she was a protestant, married to a protestant, and so had been released.

The letter also mentioned that the financial contributions from Princess Boncompagni were no longer getting through to Hulda and Ilse was investigating ways to get money to her mother. The British Red Cross, in the person of Mary Campion (the Assistant Deputy Director of the Foreign Relations Department) with whom Ilse exchanged several letters, had contacted the American Red Cross to ask them to contact the Princess. Mary had also suggested that Ilse contact the Trading with the Enemy Branch in order to obtain a licence to send financial assistance to France via the Society of Friends.[266]

---

[265] Marrus, Michel R & Paxton, Robert O. Op. cit. footnote 258, p.259-260.
[266] Letter dated 30 September 1942 from Mary Campion to Ilse Frankenbusch.

**WAR ORGANISATION**
OF THE
**BRITISH RED CROSS SOCIETY** and **ORDER OF ST. JOHN OF JERUSALEM**

President:
HER MAJESTY THE QUEEN.

Grand Prior:
H.R.H. The Duke of Gloucester, K.G.

**FOREIGN RELATIONS DEPARTMENT**

Director:
THE RT. HON. THE EARL OF CLARENDON, K.G., G.C.M.G., G.C.V.O.

TELEPHONE NOS.:
WHITEHALL 3007 & 3008

Deputy Director:
MISS S. J. WARNER, O.B.E.

Assistant Deputy Directors:
LADY ENID BROWNE
MISS MARY CAMPION, O.B.E.
MISS HELEN McSWINEY

*Warwick House*
*St. James's, S.W.I.* ~~THE LORD CHAMBERLAIN'S OFFICE ST. JAMES'S PALACE, LONDON, S.W.I.~~

PLEASE QUOTE REF. MGC/RAP
P/C.

30th September, 1942.

Miss I. Frankenbusch,
12, Silchester Court,
Thornton Heath.

Dear Miss Frankenbusch,

We have just received the following letter from the International Migration Service: -

"Following up our letter of June 17, we beg to inform you that we received a letter from our office in Lyon regarding Mrs. Frankenbusch. We are told that she had been arrested in August, but has been released, as she could prove that she was a protestant and married to a protestant. She is now back at home but her material situation is difficult and she would be very grateful if her daughter could send her assistance. Miss Frankenbusch is now living at 12, Silchester Court Thornton Heath. Could you please get in touch with her and inquire whether, as we suggested in June, she already contacted the Quakers who might help her to obtain the authorisation to send money to her mother. As we told you in June, Mrs. Frankenbusch was regularly receiving assistance from Princess Boncompagni, but it seems this is no longer thecase, since our correspondent also asks us to get in touch with Princess Boncompagni We are asking our correspondent for more precision on the matter."

As soon as I hear from Geneva, we will write again to the American Red Cross, and ask them to get in touch with Princess Boncompagni, and see if something can be done to adjust the machinery.

If you wished to send any help yourself, it would be necessary to obtain a licence from the Trading with the Enemy Branch, to send via the Society of Friends. *I think this would be granted. The address is*

*24 Kingsway.*

Yours sincerely,

*Mary G Campion*

M.G.Campion

*Letter from Mary Campion, British Red Cross about Hulda's arrest and release in August 1942.*

\*

By mid October, again in a letter from Mary Campion, it seems that Ilse was able to send payments to her mother. Mary said that if it happened that Ilse was not able to contact her mother herself then her

Branch would write to the International Red Cross to make enquiries through the *Service International D'Aide Aux Emigrants* about Hulda but as Ilse was in direct contact with her at the moment it was not necessary to do so.[267]

Also in October, Ilse receives a letter from the Trading with the Enemy Branch of the Treasury and Board of Trade informing her that the Friends Service Council of the Society of Friends have been authorised to arrange payments to Hulda 'calculated at the rate of exchange of 176.625 Frs to one pound sterling' up to an amount of 2000 francs which can be sent in a lump sum or in monthly instalments.[268] This must have been such a relief to Ilse, to know that now she is able to help her mother in some way.

*

Later in October, in a letter from the Central Agency of the Prisoners of War of the Red Cross, Hulda is informed that their efforts to trace Gisela have been unsuccessful but if they, in the future, obtain any information then they wouldn't hesitate to inform her.[269] Hulda sent a copy of this letter to Ilse when she wrote to her on the 1 November.

An undated letter from Ilse written sometime in October encourages her mother to keep her spirits up and not to lose all courage and hope. She tells Hulda that she is enjoying her new job and that she and Frank have moved into a two-roomed apartment (at 12, Silchester Court, London Road, Thornton Heath) which they have made very cosy. Now that she's not living with Aunt Irma, they are getting along a lot better and they see each other at least twice a week. Frank sends his regards.[270] Ilse is obviously more settled both in her personal life with Frank and in her job and it is a long time before she mentions again the possibility of applying for another job or moving to another address.

*

---

[267] Letter dated 13 October 1942 from Mary Campion to Ilse Frankenbusch.
[268] Letter dated 22 October 1942 from A.Sayers of the Trading with the Enemy Branch of the Treasury and Board of Trade to Ilse Frankenbusch.
[269] Letter dated 23 October 1942 from the Central Agency of Prisoners of War of the International Committee of the Red Cross to Hulda Frankenbusch.
[270] Undated letter from Ilse Frankenbusch to Hulda Frankenbusch.

Hulda received this letter on 1 November and replied immediately thanking Ilse for the money she sent which arrived around the same time. She was able to settle her debts, pay the doctor's bill and bring her rent payments up to date. She also got a payment from the Princess in the USA at the end of October.

"I will never willingly give up," she reassures Ilse, "but sometimes the circumstances are stronger than I."

She continually worries that she will share the same fate as Gisela and disappear one day – then she will be as unreachable as Gisela is at present.

She mentions that she wrote again to the Princess in the USA asking her to help her get over there and asks Ilse to write as well. She also encloses a note from the Red Cross about Anni whom she is worried about as she hasn't had a letter from her for a long time. She ends the letter with lots of questions that she expects Ilse to answer in her next letter and wishes her 'Happy Birthday' for her 27th birthday on 9 November. She sends her greetings to Frank and Irma and mentions a few snippets of news about people they know.[271]

*

A last telegram for the year comes to Ilse from Hulda via the Red Cross in mid November and sends her birthday greetings again. This was probably sent as a back-up in case the previous letter had not arrived.[272]

---

[271]Letter dated 1 November 1942 from Hulda Frankenbusch to Ilse Frankenbusch.
[272] Telegram dated 20 November 1942 from Hulda Frankenbusch (via the Red Cross) to Ilse Frankenbusch.

CLARENCE HOUSE,
ST. JAMES'S, LONDON, S.W.1

November 20th 1942.

Miss I. Frankenbusch,
12, Silchester Court,
Thronton Heath,
Surrey.

Dear Miss Frankenbusch,

We have received the following
message by cable from the International
Migration Service, Geneva :

MRS FRANKENBUSCH SENDS HER DAUGHTER
BEST BIRTHDAY WISHES THANKS FOR MONEY
AND LETTER ASKS ANSWER THROUGH ROBERT
IS WELL BUT ANXIOUS

I am so glad to be able to
send you this.

Yours sincerely,

*M.G. Campion.*

*Birthday telegram to Ilse from Hulda via the Red Cross,
November 1942*

197

*

Meanwhile, in the rest of the world, the war continues. At the beginning of the year, Hitler had spoken at the Berlin *Sportpalast*, threatening the Jews of the world with annihilation and blaming the weather for the failure of the offensive in the Soviet Union.

After months of fighting in the Far East, Singapore had surrendered to Japanese forces and Japanese aircraft had attacked Darwin in Australia's Northern Territory.

In the United Kingdom, the government had started rationing electricity, coal and gas and the clothing ration had been increased. Also in Britain, the *Luftwaffe* had begun the so-called 'Baedeker Raids' on provincial towns such as Exeter, Bath, Norwich and York.

The Battle of the Coral Sea continued in the Pacific followed by the Battle of Midway.

Molotov, the Soviet Foreign Secretay, arrived in London for high level talks with Winston Churchill and Anthony Eden. The Anglo-Soviet Treaty followed whereby the Foreign Secretaries agreed that no peace will be signed by one without the approval of the other.

Reinhard Heydrich, head of Reich Security, dies from his wounds after an attempted assassination in Prague. In reprisals, the Czech village of Lidice is burnt to the ground, all adult males and children are shot and the women are sent to concentration camps.

In the Soviet Union, The German plan to capture Stalingrad and the Caucasian oil fields begins with a massive airstrike at the end of August. By September, German troops are in the suburbs and Hitler is boasting that Stalingrad will fall. However, the Red Army fight back and encircle the city. German troops try to break through to relieve their troops holding the city, but at the end of the year the situation is still a stalemate.

In Africa, Tobruk falls to the Germans, the Battle of El Alamein is a victory for the Allies and they force the Germans to retreat. The Allies re-take Tobruk and win the battle for North Africa. Churchill made his famous speech.

"This is not the end. It is not even the beginning of the end. But it is, perhaps, the end of the beginning."

198

The first reports are emerging in the West that gas is being used to kill the Jews who are being sent to the east and in the United Kingdom leading clergymen and political figures hold a public meeting in October to express their outrage over Nazi Germany's persecution of the Jews.[273]

*

On 11 November 1942, shortly after the Allied landings in Morocco and Algeria, the German army moved into the Unoccupied Zone of southern France. At the same time, the Italians occupied eight French departments east of the Rhone including Provence and Nice. Although neither Hulda nor Ilse may have realised it at the time, it was the beginning of the end for the refugees living in the former Unoccupied Zone.

---

[273] Wikipedia. Timeline of World War II.
http://en.wikipedia.org/wiki/Timeline_of_World_War_II_(1942). Accessed 19 May 2013.

# Chapter 10

## 1942
### November
### to
### March 1944

It was March 1944 and Hulda prepared to leave Nice.

She had been in touch with the Reverend Gothie in Mens (Isere) who had found her a temporary lodging to use on her arrival there. Once there she hoped eventually to slip over the border into Switzerland and safety. It was the Reverend Metruger of the Reform Church in Nice who had provided the Reverend Gothie's address and both she and her friend Mademoiselle Moretti had put their names down for the Reform Church convoy due to leave Nice around 15 March.

This was one of many evacuation convoys organised by the town of Nice and, writing to the Reverend Gothie on 7 March, she reported that she already had a number and an appointment at the Town Hall to learn the date of her departure. The next departure was scheduled for the Friday 10 March but she didn't think she would get on that one and it would probably be the beginning of the following week. As the convoy was going from Nice to Grenoble, she had already investigated bus and train possibilities onwards from Grenoble to Clelles-Mens and then Mens.

"The convoys leave Nice at 20h.20 in the evening," writes Hulda, "and arrive in Grenoble at 7h.55 in the morning. The train leaves Grenoble at 11h.30 and arrives at Clelles-Mens at 13h.02. So if that day the bus for Mens doesn't leave in the afternoon then I will probably spend the night at Clelles unless I can find another means of transport to Mens."

In the same letter she promised to send the Reverend a card or telegram with the exact date of her departure as soon as she knew it.

"Thank you, thank you a thousand times," she ends the letter. "I will do everything to make sure you do not regret having given me your help and advice."[274]

By this time she knew that Mademoiselle Moretti was seriously ill with bronchitis and wouldn't be able to travel with her but if necessary Hulda was determined to travel on her own as she knew it was imperative that she leave Nice as soon as possible.

*

---

[274] Letter dated 28 February 1944 from Hulda Frankenbusch to Reverend Gothie.

The last six months had simply been a matter of survival for Hulda and with hindsight she now knew that the ten months before that of relative calm during the Italian occupation had merely been the calm before the storm.

It had been on 11 November 1942, shortly after the Allied landings in Morocco and Algeria, that the German army had moved into the Unoccupied Zone of southern France. At the same time, the Italians had occupied eight French departments east of the Rhone including Provence and Nice. In the German zone, the French police continued their manhunts for foreign Jews, while the Nazis watched on. In the Italian zone, arrests ceased and Jews already captured but not deported were released. Jews in the Italian zone found themselves better off than before the Italian occupation.

The Italian occupying forces also refused to allow labour camps in their zone as well as forbidding the stamping of identification papers or ration books with the word 'Jew' as required by a recent French law. Reports of Italian policies towards Jews spread rapidly and thousands of refugees fled into the Italian zone. Most headed towards Nice where they received the necessary residence permits and ration cards and then, from there, moved on to other areas. By the end of summer 1943, 30,000 Jews were crowded along thirty kilometres of coast in the Alpes-Maritime.[275]

*

For Jews who had been keeping a low profile from the Nazis for years, living in the Italian zone now seemed almost like freedom. Lucie Kupefer Munzer had moved from Paris to Nice with her husband Hans in 1940.

"The city is a kind of haven for Jews in France," she reported in 1943, "because the Italians, who have occupied this area, leave us alone. We have three synagogues in Nice, a kosher Jewish kitchen and many Jewish doctors."[276]

---

[275] Zuccotti, Susan. The Italians and the Holocaust: persecution, rescue and survival. NY, Basic Books, 1987, pp. 82-84.
[276] United States Holocaust Memorial Museum. Holocaust Encyclopedia. http://www.ushmm.org/wlc/idcard.php?ModuleId=10006443. Accessed 21 January 2009.

Another young refugee, Alfred Feldman also noted that in Saint-Martin-Vesubie, 40 kilometres north of Nice

"Jews pass peacefully along the street, sit in the cafes, speak in French, German and even Yiddish. Everything seems to be happening freely, there are no particular regulations and discussion flourishes with the greatest liberty."[277]

*

Meanwhile, just down the coast in Marseille in German-held territory the deportations continued and in a big operation at the end of January 1943, 1500 people were arrested and deported. Raymond-Raoul Lambard describes what he saw there.

"They had no water, no food, not a bench to sit on. Two Germans and two mobile guards were assigned to each car, cars that were sealed at departure. Acts of brutality were observed as the train departed."[278]

*

Back in Nice, despite the benign Italian occupation, Hulda's life revolved around her lack of funds, finding enough to eat, paying for her accommodation, and, in November 1942, trying to keep warm as autumn gave way to winter. By this stage of the war shortages were the norm and goods in the shops had dwindled to the mere basics. In order to survive Hulda usually spent the morning queuing for food and other essentials – not only for herself but also for others who were older and not as strong as she was. Her former life in Nice of coffee shops, visits to the cinema and shopping for gifts for Ilse seemed like a dream now despite the fact that it was only two and a half years ago. Now, her financial situation as it was, all she could do was stand outside, gaze in through the windows and remember the good times.

Staunch Protestant as she was, she attended church regularly and depended heavily on the Christian community in Nice for support in these difficult times. As she had in Paris she also gained most of her mental and cultural stimulation from the organ music and choral singing in church. At these times she was lifted out of herself and for a short time could forget real life with its poverty, hunger and cold and

---

[277] United States Holocaust Memorial Museum. Ibid. footnote 276.
[278] Lambard, Raymond-Raoul. Diary of a witness: 1940-1943. NY, Ivan R. Dee in association with the United states Holocaust Memorial Museum, 2007, p.169.

soar with the voices and be part of the joy of the Christian message. Taking part in worship lifted her morale and for a while she could take home with her the comfort of being part of a small group of like-minded individuals who were all trying to survive the present and look forward to the future with a certain amount of hope. Every Sunday as she took the short walk to her local church, her heart lifted and it stayed that way during the walk back to her single room at the *pension*.

*

It was after the Italian occupation that communications with the outside world became even more difficult. Very few letters were getting through and telegrams had to go via a third party, usually the International Red Cross, the Quakers or the International Migration Centre in Geneva. The frustration and anxiety of both Hulda and Ilse can only be imagined. More so for Hulda as she always felt herself to be living on the edge, trying to keep a low profile and concentrating on living just one day at a time. News from family and friends outside the country was her lifeline and gave her a reason to survive. At least Ilse had made a life of sorts for herself with Frank and a job that she enjoyed.

*

Up until November 1942 Ilse had been able to send money to France but eventually this became impossible and a letter from Mary Campion of the British Red Cross in December of that year, said that they had received word that Hulda had not received any money from the Princess Boncompagni since July but had received 700 Francs from Ilse via the Quakers which had been very opportune as she had been in a desperate and nervous state. This was the last sum of money that Ilse was able to send to Hulda but Mary Campion said she would contact the American Red Cross and ask them to get in touch with the Princess in the hope that she may still be able to send money from the US.

Unfortunately, this doesn't seem to have worked as a message from Hulda to Ilse in February 1943, again via the Red Cross, says that she hasn't heard from the Princess since November and is now having to sell some of her belongings and live off charity. This confirms a letter from the American Red Cross in the same month, saying that at that time it wasn't possible to transmit funds to enemy-occupied territory

206

from the US and Princess Boncompagni had been informed of this fact.[279]

Both Ilse and Anni continued to investigate all avenues to try and help their mother and maintain contact via the Red Cross. In a telegram at the beginning of February, Ilse reports that Alice (her cousin) has had a baby boy, the first of the next generation of the extended family and welcome news after Anni's miscarriage in 1942.[280] It was in reply to this telegram that Hulda mentioned that she had had an accident and burned her leg which had left her very sick and weak. She said she was better now but without money as she had sold nearly everything she owned. Anni, meanwhile, had been contacted by the International Migration Service in Geneva in March, asking if there was any way she could help her mother.[281] Ilse, around the same time, had obviously approached 'Mr Secretary Eden' at the Foreign Office because she received a reply in early April 1943 reiterating that it was impossible to transfer funds either 'directly or through a neutral intermediary'.

---

[279] Letter dated 26 February 1943 from Philip E Ryan, American Red Cross to Mary Campion, British Red Cross.
[280] Telegram dated 8 February 1943 from Ilse Frankenbusch to Hulda Frankenbusch.
[281] Letter dated 19 March 1943 from International Migration Service, Geneva to Anita Heniger.

In any further communication
on this subject, please quote

No. W 5076/49/48
and address—
*not to any person by name*
but to—
" The Under-Secretary of State,"
Foreign Office,
London, S.W.1.

FOREIGN OFFICE.

S.W.1.

8th April, 1943.

Madam,

    With reference to your letter of 31st January regarding your desire to arrange remittances for the support of Mrs. Hilda Frankenbusch at Nice, I am directed by Mr. Secretary Eden to inform you that the competent authorities are not prepared to allow transfers of funds across the exchanges, either directly or through a neutral intermediary. It is regretted, therefore, that no steps can be taken on your behalf in this matter.

    2.  I am to add that, as Mrs. Frankenbusch is a Czechoslovak citizen, it is open to you to approach the Czechoslovak Ministry of Finance, 35, Furzecroft, Brown Street, W.1.

             I am,
                  Madam,
           Your obedient Servant,

Miss I. Frankenbusch,
    12, Silchester Court,
      London Road,
        Thornton Heath,
          Surrey.

*Letter from the Foreign Office to Ilse, April 1943.*

    The writer suggests that, as Hulda is a Czechoslovak citizen, Ilse could approach the Czechoslovak Ministry of Finance in London.[282] This Ilse immediately did but, again, was informed after a couple of months that they, too, were unable to help.

*

---

[282]  Letter dated 8 April 1943 from the Foreign Office, London to Ilse Frankenbusch.

There are only three letters from Hulda in 1943 that have survived – two (plus a short excerpt from another) are addressed to Alex (Sani). The first was written in June and thanks him for his news of Anni and Wim. His letter was the first Hulda had received from him in over a year and for her it was like being reconnected to the outside world.

"Your letter gives me again a little hope," she says, "and of that I have very little."

This letter to Sani tells us in detail what her life was like. She has had no word from 'Margarete' [the Princess] for eight months and any connection with her or her bank has been cut off. In the first few weeks of the year she had very little to eat and then she began selling whatever possessions she could find a market for. Now she lives in her 'nearly empty apartment' and exists with the support of a 'relief organisation.' However their funds are in short supply and are often irregular so that she often has to go hungry.

"If you were to see me now!" she says, " I have lost 19kg, am like an emaciated skeleton and have become quite an old woman!"

She also gives more details about her accident in March when she severely burnt her left leg. She had no money to go to a doctor so handled it herself with 'household remedies' which resulted in a severe blood infection that confined her to the house for two months. Since then the 'relief organisation' has paid for a doctor and also for the medication she has needed.

"I need help quickly," she says, "I am really at the end of my resistance and very depressed and under great strain!"

She mentions her mother and the anxiety of not having heard from her for eighteen months. She gets news from Ilse via the Red Cross from time to time and hopes that all the family can just survive a little longer.

"The depression, the huge loneliness and the sense of loss weighs very heavily on me," she writes, "and I have a continual sense of waiting to be uprooted."

"I am ruled by one thought," she says. "will I be alive in the morning."

All her former optimism has disappeared and everything now seems black and gloomy.[283]

*

Taking into consideration the amount of time it took for letters to arrive at their destination at that time, it seems that Sani must have replied quite quickly as the next letter to him was in early September. She says what a joy it was to receive his letter and that it was like a call from another world.

"A world that no longer exists," writes Hulda, "that lies so far in the past, that one can no longer understand that one once lived in such a world!"

She thanks him for news of Anni and Wim and has received money from them with which she paid off some pressing debts and bought some food. She's a lot more positive in this letter and says she is busy from morning to night. In the morning she goes to the shop and stands in the queue for other people.

"In the afternoon," she says, "I'm a companion, teacher, secretary and also a bit of a nurse to an old Dutchman who is mean and very unappetizing."

Twice a week, when she has an hour or two to spare, she bathes in the sea or walks into town to spend time 'people-watching' in the coffee houses or shops. For almost a year she has not been in a cinema or coffee house but she gets some comfort from looking at them from the outside.

"Oh Sani," she says, "sometimes I am so despondent. My usual good optimism has forsaken me and my situation, grief, poverty and deprivation have made a thorough mess of me."

She persuades herself that she must survive and not lose courage. When she looks after herself, dresses properly and has something to eat, then everything seems less hopeless. However sometimes she is hungry and feels weak.

"Then," she says, "maybe it is not so surprising that I get depressed."

---

[283] Letter dated 6 June 1943 from Hulda Frankenbusch to Alex [Sani Volnay/Torday].

She sends her greetings to Rudi and hopes they'll all be together once again.

"You dear Alex" she writes at the end of the letter, "I thank once again for your dear lines, and send you many, many heartfelt greetings."[284]

*

Six days after writing this letter, on 9th September 1943, the Nazis entered Nice.

The Italians had provided the people of Nice with only a brief respite. During the ten months the Italians had been in control there, their protection of the Jews in their zone had enraged the Nazis and the German Foreign Ministry had exerted considerable pressure on them to deliver refugees for deportation. For the next few months there seems to have been a stand-off between the two powers with Mussolini promising the Germans one thing and his officials based in Nice doing another. However, Italian authorities realised that some action was necessary to appease German wrath and embarked on a policy to send Jews away from the coast to enforced residency in the interior.[285] The Germans were not impressed.

Mussolini's fall in July 1943 did not alter things in Nice for over a month but the new government was in secret negotiations with the Allies about an armistice. Anticipating this, they decided in August to withdraw from most of occupied France, holding on to only a vastly reduced area around Nice. On 28 August, Italian officials agreed that the Jews should be allowed to accompany the army when it withdrew and a convoy of trucks was hired to bring refugees from Haute Savoy back to Nice and, it was hoped, safety. Following on from this, Angelo Donati, an Italian Jew from Modena, who had been at the forefront of refugee assistance activities in Nice since 1940, organised a massive rescue effort.

He knew that thousands of Jews could not remain permanently in the area around Nice, soon to be practically surrounded by Germans and dependent on the Italian army for their protection. During the last week of August and the first week of September, he made a huge

---

[284] Letter dated 9 September 1943 from Hulda Frankenbusch to Alex [Sani Volnay/Torday].

[285] Zuccotti, Susan. Op.cit. footnote 275, p. 85.

effort to save his people. By the morning of 8 September he had negotiated a deal with the Italian government, British and US representatives at the Vatican and the American Joint Distribution Committee. The Italian government would supply four ships, the British and Americans agreed to let 30,000 refugees land in North Africa and the Committee agreed to finance the whole thing. The armistice was not due to be made public until the end of September and it was planned that the ships would have sailed well before then.[286]

*

The premature announcement of the armistice caught everyone, except the Germans, totally unprepared. The plan had to be abandoned and with the Germans advancing quickly, the Italians knew they couldn't hold Nice and retreated back across the border leaving the Jews in Nice totally unprotected.

The Nazis were determined to take revenge for the ten months of Italian interference with their Final Solution and the Jews in Nice were caught up in the most ruthless manhunt of the war in Western Europe. For over a week every boarding house and hotel in the city and every train leaving the city was searched. 1,800 people were rounded up and sent to Drancy, the notorious French holding camp on the outskirts of Paris. From there the trains left for Auschwitz.[287]

*

Panic reigned in Nice amongst the Jews but Hulda managed to survive, whether it was with the help of the Christian community is not known but the church certainly played an ever-increasing part in her life from then on. The British Red Cross was still passing on messages between Hulda and Ilse and it was a letter from them to Ilse in late September that passed on the news that Hulda was giving private lessons and during June was able to earn 300-400 Francs.[288]

[286] Zuccotti, Susan. Op. cit. footnote 275, pp. 86-87.
[287] Zuccotti, Susan. Op cit. Footnote 275, pp. 88-89.
[288] Letter dated 21 September 1943 from F. Revelstoke, British Red Cross to Ilse Frankenbusch.

**WAR ORGANISATION**
of the
**BRITISH RED CROSS SOCIETY and ORDER OF ST. JOHN OF JERUSALEM**

**FOREIGN RELATIONS DEPARTMENT**
*Chairman :*
MAJ.-GENERAL SIR JOHN KENNEDY, K.B.E., C.B., C.M.G., D.S.O.

*Director:*
MISS S. J. WARNER, O.B.E.

TELEPHONE No.:
ABBEY 2511/5

Allied Prisoners of War Packing Centre
Heads of Packing Centre:
MRS. GRAZEBROOK
MRS. SECKER

PLEASE QUOTE REF.    DW Cz

CLARENCE HOUSE,
ST. JAMES'S, LONDON, S.W.1

September 21st, 1943.

Miss Frankenbusch,
12, Silchester Court,
London Road,
Thornton Heath, Surrey.

Dear Miss Frankenbusch,

We have just received a letter from the International Migration Service at Geneva and think it
best to let you have a copy.    It is:-
re:- Hilda FRANKENBUSCH.
"We beg to inform you that we just receive a
report from our office in France on the above
mentioned case.
We are told thatit was possible for them to
help Mrs. Frankenbusch regularly during the
last months.    Her case was also referred to
a protestant committee in Nice which gave her
the moral help she needed.    Mrs.Franken-
busch's health is still bad.    In her last
letter, dated July 16th, she informed our
office, that it was possible for her to give
some private lessons and that she was able
to earn Fr.300 - Fr.400. during the month
of June.    She was very glad of it.
Will you please forward these news to Miss
Frankenbusch. Our office does not tell us,
if Mrs. Frankenbusch received the messages
from her daughter, but we hope that the latter
received in the meantime directly news from her
mother!"

We are very sorry that your mother's health is
still bad, but are so glad thatshe has been receiving
help which must be a great relief to you.

Yours sincerely,

*Anriot C M Palmer.*

for F.Revelstoke.

*Letter from the Red Cross to Ilse*
*giving news of Hulda, September 1943.*

213

*

There exists a short excerpt from a letter to Sani written in November 1943 which shows her desperation at that time and deserves to be quoted in full:

"I do not know anyone here who can help me," says Hulda. "Our local pastor, who is very kind and helpful, hopes to be able to recommend somewhere to me. That will be determined today or tomorrow, but that does not mean I can stay there and there is not enough time. Everything has happened too quickly. And there is no money! Now hunger and affliction will really begin. And I am very tired! And no message from Ilse! These worries! All my love to Anni and Wim. The thought of them and Ilse keeps me going. I want to see them again, them and my grandchild!"[289] [Anni was pregnant again by then and the baby was due in May 1944].

The last letter, also written in November, is addressed to Johani, she starts by apologising for her strange handwriting – she is writing in bed with her gloves on as the temperature in the room is only five degrees. She is paying full board to live in a bathroom in which her only furniture is a sofa bed and a table with two stools. The bath is in one corner without a copper and the room has a stone floor, looks north and is unheated because the gas has been cut off.

"This is how I live," she says, "this is how I live, this is how I live day after day."

Luckily she is not at home much as she has a lot to do and every afternoon she is with her old Dutchman. She tells Johani that his name is Mendes and his father was the founder of an old Dutch banking firm of the same name and asks him whether the name and bank are known to him.

She talks about Anni and Wim, with whom Johani is in contact and of whom he has given Hulda news. She is very glad that they are united and happy as she had been concerned that 'these difficult times' might have had a detrimental effect on their marriage. She says she had always wanted to be a grandmother and now it seems she will be.

---

[289]  Excerpt from letter dated 26 November 1943 from Hulda Frankenbusch to Sani Volnay/Torday.

"This letter ought to come to you near Christmas, so I wish you now a truly happy celebration and a happy and peaceful 1944" she ends the letter. "Perhaps, perhaps a year of peace? God give us! Please tell Anni and Wim that my thoughts will be with them and that I wish them everything good and lovely. They must also in the new year remember me and not forget me."[290]

*

There is a brief telegram from Hulda to Ilse in early January 1944, saying she hasn't had any news from her and is anxious about her. She tells her that Sani has seen Anni who is expecting a baby.[291]During the early months of 1944 the Christian churches in Nice helped a lot of their refugee members plan their departure from Nice which was

*Telegram from Hulda to Ilse, January 1944.*

---

290 Letter dated 28 November 1943 from Hulda Frankenbusch to Johani.
291 Telegram date 4 January 1944 from Hulda Frankenbusch to Ilse Frankenbusch.

becoming an increasingly dangerous place to live for people like Hulda who in their hearts were Christian but in the minds of the Nazis were Jewish. After her letters to the Reverend Gothie and his reassurances that a lodging had been found for her in Mens, Hulda knew that it was only a matter of time before she was assigned a date and the number of the convoy on which she would leave. She had already packed the few items that she would take with her. All her worldly possessions fitted into a trunk, a suitcase, a basket and a hatbox which now sat in her room ready to go. On the day of the convoy's departure all she had to do was close them, call a taxi and get to the station.

On Monday 13 March she heard that she would be leaving on the Wednesday and sent a quick telegram to the Reverend Gothie to let him know.[292] She was very hopeful, despite the fact that she was having to uproot herself once again. She finally felt that there could be a future for her in the small community of Mens and possibly outside France. On Wednesday 15 March 1944, she arrived at the station early as she knew it would take some time to register her luggage and make sure it was all loaded onto the train. Once this was done she walked along the platform looking for her assigned carriage and seat. She was about to board the train when she was stopped, her documents inspected and she was arrested by the Gestapo officers who were checking passengers on every train that left Nice.

*

A plaque commemorating the 3,000 Jews who were deported from Nice railway station can be found there today.

*

Despite her protestations, she would have been taken to an assembly point where there was already a group of other detainees. From here she was probably taken to a holding camp in southern France as, from documents that exist, it is known that there were 10 days between her arrest and her arrival at Drancy. In this camp she would have been questioned and processed before being moved on to Drancy on the outskirts of Paris. By this time she may have suspected that her final destination was that gate with the words *Arbeit Macht Frei* over it, the entrance to Auschwitz.

---

[292] Telegram dated 13 March 1944 from Hulda Frankenbusch to Reverend Gothie.

On the 31st of August 1942, 554 Jews, including about twenty children, who lived in the regions of the Maritime Alps, the lower Alps and Monaco, were arrested on the orders of the Vichy Government and handed over to the Gestapo.
After being grouped together at the Auvare military base, they were taken by train from the Saint-Roch station to the camp at Drancy in the occupied zone and from there they were deported to Auschwitz.
Between the 10th of September 1943 and the 30th of July 1944, more than 3,000 Jews, including about 300 children, were arrested by the Gestapo in the Maritime Alps, the lower Alps and Monaco and deported to Auschwitz after having been transferred from the Central Station in Nice to the camp at Drancy.
Almost all those deported were assassinated: less than 3% survived.

*English translation of the plaque.*

\*

Her luggage continued on to Mens without her and the Reverend Gothie looked after it until the end of the war. It was in a letter from Mademoiselle Moretti in April that he discovered what had happened to Hulda.[293]

A telegram from Ilse to Hulda written in May, addressed to Hulda's old address in Nice, was forwarded on to the Reverend in Mens and it was from him, in a letter written in October, that she first found out about Hulda's arrest.[294]

---

[293] Letter dated 5 April 1944 from Mlle Moretti to Reverend Gothie.
[294] Letter dated 16 October 1944 from Reverend Gothie to Ilse Frankenbusch.

**5th April 1944**

36 rue Herold, Nice

Dear Reverend
I am sorry to be so late in thanking you for your
nice, comforting letter but I have had bronchitis
and have been quite ill. The doctor hopes that I
could travel at the end of April so I hope to arrive
about the 30th or during the first week of May.
I will be so happy to see you, as you have been
so kind as to concern yourself with me and I will
also be happy to take the room and kitchen for
180fr which you have so kindly found for me. I
repeat, I hope to be useful in some way.
Thank you for keeping the luggage of Madame
Frankenbusch, my poor friend was arrested by
the Gestapo and in spite of all my efforts to find
out, I do not know where they have taken her.

My sincere good wishes for the most beautiful
celebration of the year, that of Jesus Christ, with
my greatest thanks and see you soon.

Moretti

*Letter from Mlle Moretti to Reverend Gothie telling of*
*Hulda's arrest by the Gestapo, April 1944*

Ilse continued to write to various organisations in an effort to find
out what had happened to her mother and it was in a letter from the
Czechoslovak Red Cross in April 1945 that she learned that Hulda had
been deported to Auschwitz via Drancy.[295] Once she knew this Ilse

---

[295]  Letter dated 26 April 1945 from Marina Pauliny, Czechoslovak Red Cross to Ilse
Frankenbusch.

approached the USSR Embassy in London who referred her on to the Polish Embassy.[296] They wrote that a list of Jewish survivors in Poland was being compiled and this would be distributed to Jewish organisations in the UK who will inform her when it is completed. The letter from the Polish Embassy also notes:

"Since millions of Jews were murdered in Poland by the Germans, it is practically impossible to find your relatives, for in most cases the trace [sic] of those murdered is lost."[297]

*

This must have seemed like a dead end to Ilse – there was nothing more she could do except wait and hope. The Czechoslovak Red Cross had informed her that it would be impossible for Hulda's belongings to be sent from France to England until after the war, so, again, all she could do was wait. It wasn't until April 1946 that she wrote again to the Reverend Gothie asking him to open the luggage and describe to her what was inside so she could decide which of her mother's belongings she wanted to be sent to her in England.

The Reverend replied:

"Firstly, I want to say how much sympathy I felt as I was doing it [opening Hulda's luggage], both for your poor, dear mother and for you who grieve for her. It is you who should have been opening her baggage and the trunk she had prepared thinking she was coming here when she was evacuated from Nice. These things she must have missed so much in her horrid detention through Nazi brutality. Is it possible? Now that one knows the details of these atrocious camps. How dreadful humanity can be when hate takes over. Oh, we really need to spread the love of Lord Jesus.

I have therefore opened your mother's luggage but am rather embarrassed at having to describe the contents to you. First there are a lot of ordinary things like bottles of perfume, full or empty, a small set of cooking pans, a little perishable food (all evidently things which would have been useful in her daily life once she was installed, but

---

[296] Letter dated 8 May 1945 from the Embassy of the Union of Soviet Socialist Republics to Ilse Frankenbusch.

[297] Letter dated 26 May 1945 from the Provisional Government of the Polish Republic to Ilse Frankenbusch.

evidently of no value to you). There are also two pairs of spectacles. Then there are quite a few dresses, coats, blouses, three pairs of shoes and a profusion of gloves. There are also several fans, some hats, feathers and belts. In all that there are surely some things you would like to have.

There are also books, almost all of which are school books about learning foreign languages (not very interesting I think). There are also quite a lot of newspaper cuttings and guides to the towns in which she has lived: Vienna in Austria, Fiume, Paris, Nice (these also seem to me to be of little interest).

As for photos, I have only found those which I enclose with this letter, and as for correspondence, I am sending a first package separately. You will let me know if you receive it. Then I will send you a second package. I will also enquire if there is a possibility of sending things via the Red Cross.'[298]

In this way, this gentle, considerate man described the remnants of Hulda's life as a refugee in France.

*

Three months after Hulda's arrest, on 6 June 1944, came the Allied landings on the Normandy beaches, thus opening a second front against the Germans. Two months later and exactly five months to the day after Hulda's arrest, on 15 August 1944, Nice was liberated. Allied forces from North Africa landed in southern France and advanced rapidly northeast. Ten days later Allied troops reached Paris and by the end of the year most of France, Belgium and Holland were liberated and the Germans were in retreat.[299]

How tragic it was that after staying one step ahead of the Nazis for six years since the *Anschluss* and surviving in Nice for so long, Hulda was not able to stay alive for another five months.

---

[298] Letter dated April 1946 from Reverend Gothie to Ilse Frankenbusch.
[299] United States Holocaust Memorial Museum. World War II: Timeline. http://www.ushmm.org/wlc/en/article.php?ModuleId=10007306.

# Chapter 11

## The Conclusion

Hulda arrived at *Camp de Drancy* on the 24 March 1944 according to a list of deportees - see document number 7 on the photo pages at the end of this chapter (pages236-237). This document also notes that she will beleaving on convoy No.71. On her arrival papers - see documentnumber 6 on the photo pages - it was recorded that the sum of '*mille six cent quatre vingt francs*' (Fr.frs 1680) and a gold bracelet was received from Mme Hulda Frankenbusch of 6 *Rue Francois Aune*, Nice. Her identification number was 17538. This document was dated 31 March 1944.

..

\*

Drancy internment camp, located in a northeastern suburb of Paris, 7kms from the centre of the city, was a U-shaped building as can be seen in an aerial photo at number 2 on the photo pages. It was constructed in the 1930s, and served as a police barracks before the war.[300] French police enclosed the barracks and courtyard with a barbed-wire fence and provided the guards for the camp.[301] It was one of many in France built to house those escaping the Spanish Civil War and Jewish refugees.

When it first came into use it fell under the command of the Gestapo Office of Jewish Affairs in France and German SS Captain Theodor Danneker. In July 1943 Alois Brunner became Camp Commandant. He removed French guards from the interior of the camp and replaced them with SS guards.[302] It was Alois Brunner who, in August 1942, had been responsible for the round-up and arrest of Jews in Nice and surrounding regions.

\*

Drancy was in the middle of a community of 35,000 people,[303] many of whom could see directly into the camp and could at least guess the conditions in which the inmates were living. It appears that people were afraid to talk about what was going on in their midst in

---

[300]  United States Holocaust Memorial Museum. Holocaust Encyclopedia. Drancy. http://www.ushmm.org/wlc/en/article.php?ModuleId=10005215. Accessed 25 May 2013.
[301]  Ibid. footnote 300.
[302]  Marrus, Michael. Vichy France and the Jews. Stanford University Press, 1995. Pp. 253-4.
[303]  Drancy: a concentration camp in Paris, 1941-1944. Director: Stephen Trombley. DVD.

case they were denounced by their neighbours and sent to join the inmates. In the days of the occupation the ordinary people of Paris lived in fear. It wasn't that they were indifferent to what was happening in the camp, just frightened.

*

The building had huge rooms without partitions and inmates were housed 50 to a room. They had bunk beds but no mattresses and were forced to sleep on bare boards. There was no privacy involved with life in Drancy and inmates were forced to undress in front of others and made to feel inferior.[304] To a strict Jew this would have been particularly shameful and even to someone like Hulda, Christian as she was, it would have been extremely painful.

*

The SS and the gendarmes were responsible for the security and discipline of the camp but the prisoners ran the internal organization themselves. To understand how this worked it is important to realize that there were two classes of Jews in France.

The French-born Jews had become part of the old established French middle class but the foreign-born Jews, more recently arrived from Eastern Europe, were mostly working class and left wing.[305] Hulda, because of her origins, would have been classed as foreign-born despite the fact that she was neither working class nor left wing.

*

The building at Drancy was divided by 22 staircases that separated and allowed access to the rooms. The inmates elected a 'Head of Staircase', usually a French-born Jew, who was responsible for giving out food, roll calls and helping people wherever possible. The French-born Jews were given the administrative and organizational positions, while the foreigners had the more menial chores such as sweeping out the rooms and cleaning the toilets.[306] The only toilet facility was a latrine at one end of the compound to service 5000 people.

*

---

[304] Ibid. footnote 303.
[305] Drancy: a concentration camp in Paris, 1941-1944. Op.cit. footnote 303.
[306] Drancy: a concentration camp in Paris, 1941-1944. Op.cit. footnote 303.

It was in these surroundings and conditions that Hulda spent the next three weeks, never knowing what the next day would bring, trying to survive from one day to the next and hoping against hope that the war would end before her number came up. Photo number 3 in the photo pages shows a general view of Drancy Camp.

She was assigned to a staircase, living in close proximity with 50 other people, sleeping on bare boards, eating the meager rations and exercising in the courtyard when this was allowed. Mostly keeping her head down in the hope that she would not be noticed by the SS. The 50 people in her room would have been constantly changing as some departed and others replaced them.

*

Early graffitti in Drancy shows that many inmates did not know where they were going and wrote that they were leaving in good spirits. To begin with, the fiction that they were going to 'workcamps' was plausible but once deportations of the elderly, the sick and children began, this was clearly unbelievable. Then deportees coined a word 'Pitchipol' (somewhere) to describe where they were going.[307]

*

Inevitably Hulda's luck eventually ran out and, on the 12 April 1944, she was assigned to the 'Departure' staircase. Here there were no bunks, only straw on the ground,[308] and it was here that she spent her last night in Drancy.

Roll call was at 5am next morning and together with her fellow deportees, she would have been loaded onto buses, each bus including an SS guard with a machine gun. By 6am the last bus would have departed, taking its load of human cargo to the railway station which at this hour would have been deserted and lit by search lights.

*

Hulda left Drancy on 13 April 1944 to be transported to Auschwitz Concentration Camp on Convoy 71. The details on the document that record her departure – document number 9 on the photo pages – gives

---

[307] Drancy: a concentration camp in Paris, 1941-1944. Op.cit. footnote 303.
[308] Drancy: a concentration camp in Paris, 1941-1944. Op.cit. footnote 303.

the date,her reference number, her last name (Frankenbusch nee Kerber) her first name, her date and place of birth, her nationality (Czech), her profession and her place of abode in France.

In Convoy 71 there were 1,500 deportees including 624 men, 854 women and 22 'indetermines'.[309] A second list of deportees, see document number 8 in the photo pages, lists Hulda as no. 372 and gives her date of birth, 'hotelier' as her profession and her reference number, 17538.

There were 148 children under 12 years and 295 under 19 years. One group of 34 children were arrested at Izieu by the chief of the Gestapo at Lyon, Klaus Barbie.[310] Simone Jacob, now Simone Veil was found in this transportation. She was under 16 years old and was one of the youngest survivors of the deportations from France.

The fact that Hulda was part of Convoy 71 from Drancy to Auschwitz is the last official information that can be found concerning the life and death of Hulda Frankenbusch, nee Kerber.

*

From other accounts it is possible to piece together what the journey to Auschwitz was like. All the deportees would have been taken to the Paris-Bobigny station, the station nearest to Drancy. Hulda, along with all the others, would have been lined up and loaded onto a cattle wagon. There would have been much pushing and shoving and she would probably have needed assistance to get up into the wagon.

She would have been in the depths of despair but there would have been others in a similar situation to her, older single women with no family, who might have offered some support. There could also have been orphaned children on board and she might have been able to temporarily forget her own plight and focus on them and give them some comfort.

Being an intelligent and well-read woman, there is no doubt that she knew exactly where she was going and that this was going to be her final journey.

*

---

[309] Documents provided by the Red Cross International Tracing Service.
[310] United States Holocaust Memorial Museum. Op.cit. footnote 300.

By 1944, the numbers being deported were dropping and the overcrowding in the wagon might not have been as great as previously. There were probably around 70-80 people in a space where 50 would have been too many. There could have been a bucket for people to relieve themselves into and possibly also a container of water.[311]

The doors to the wagon would have been rolled shut, the heavy bolts pushed into position with a grinding noise and locked. For the majority of the people inside that would become their world for the next two days.

Those who had managed to get a position near the small window would have been able to watch the changing landscape and breathe fresh air. The down side was that it was colder near the windows and although spring was in the air in April 1944, the nights would have still been cold.

*

With a sudden jerk the train would have moved off probably throwing its living cargo off balance and once they had steadied themselves it's possible they may have organized themselves to take turns sitting and standing. There would have been no room for lying down.

For the older people like Hulda, sick and weak as she was, the next two days would have been a living nightmare. She was probably held up by the people next to her and may even have lapsed into unconsciousness at times still standing and not able to fall.

*

The train would have increased in speed as it left the city and moved into open country and would have rushed past farms, villages and towns, all evidence of another world that she was no longer part of. The day could have been a bright, cool spring day but inside the wagon the air was probably hot and heavy with the crush of bodies. Hulda probably felt claustrophobic and unbearably tired, numb with fear and panic, knowing that she was going to her death.

The train would have continued to rush on to its destination, its cargo now silent, each person probably locked inside their own world,

---

[311]  Biderman, Abraham. The world of my past. Random House, 1995. pp.191-2.

staring aimlessly into space with empty eyes. Each face most likely bearing the marks of hunger, pain and weariness.

Hulda might have retreated into memories of happier times, growing up in Vienna with her mother Gisela, the early years of her marriage to Rudolf and her two children, Anita and Ilse. She would have been glad that Anita and Ilse had survived and that another generation of the family was on its way because Anita was pregnant with what would be Hulda's first grandchild, due to arrive next month. The family would continue and she would be remembered.

*

The journey would have gone on and on as the death train, with its repetitious clatter of the wheels, sped into the dark of one night, through another long day and into a second night, the hours and minutes seemingly endless. The rhythmical noise of the wheels dulling the senses of the inmates and continuously reminding them of where they were traveling to and what their fate would be.

In the afternoon of the second day, the train would have started to slow down as it went through a small station, dimly lit and unattended. A sign would have appeared in big black letters on a white oblong board with a black border: 'Auschwitz'.[312]

The people at the windows would have let everyone else know what was happening and the fear and panic within the wagon would have increased with people weeping, crying out and praying.

The train would have rolled along ever more slowly, branching off from the main line across flat fields covered with grass and the occasional lonely birch tree able to be seen through the small window. This part of Auschwitz was called Brzezinki – derived from the Polish word 'brzozy', meaning birches. In German it was called Birkenau.[313]

*

The brakes would have been applied more heavily and there would probably have been the loud squealing of metal against metal and a banging of heavy steel as the buffers struck one another bringing the train to a halt and throwing its cargo off balance again. Exhausted, they could have fallen, one on top of the other.

---

[312]  Bideman, Abraham. Op.cit. footnote 311,    p. 193.
[313]  Bideman, Abraham. Op.cit. footnote 311,    p. 193.

Fear could have filled Hulda's heart, causing the blood to rush to her head and hammer into a blinding headache. Her heart would be racing in a panic attack and having a weak heart anyway, she would be wondering if she was about to have a heart attack or a stroke. There would have been absolutely nothing she could do about it and in the hopelessness of her situation she may have hoped to die there on the floor of the wagon, crushed by the people around her and on top of her.

In her weakened state it is entirely possible that she died during the journey and there are no records to tell us otherwise.

*

If she survived, the next thing she would have known would have been the doors of the cattle wagon being unlocked with the grinding noise of the heavy metal bolts. The doors would have been rolled wide open and hell would have broken loose with shouts of '*Raus! Raus! Schnell! Schnell!*'[314]

The screaming and crying would have been deafening as people scrambled from the wagons, being helped on their way with rifle butts, truncheons and sticks while the Germans pushed and shouted. The crowd would have been in a panic, herding together, with the old and the sick falling and being trampled underfoot.

The SS would have separated the women from the men, the children going with their mothers and the old and sick being kept apart. The Germans would have been brutal and savage, continuing their beating and shouting.

The barking of the watch dogs and the lamenting and wailing would have been wringing in Hulda's ears and the wild scenes around her would make her think she had descended into a living hell.

All around were barbed wire fences, watch towers, search lights and guards at regular intervals surrounding the crowd. Barracks lined up in rows stretching into the distance, seemingly for many miles.

*

The new arrivals would have been formed into long queues slowly moving towards a group of SS officers. Photo number 1 in the photo

---

[314] Bideman, Abraham. Op.cit. footnote 311, p. 202.

pages shows the queues waiting for selection. One of the SS involved in making the selection could have been an immaculately dressed officer wearing white gloves who would have pointed with his finger left, right, left, right.   To his left was death, to his right was life. This would have been Dr Joseph Mengele, Auschwitz's 'Angel of Death'.[315]

Hulda, being an older woman, sick and weak, would most likely have been pointed to the left. There was nothing to do except follow the person in front of her, maybe assist someone weaker than herself, and walk to her death.

She was 54 years old and in a different age could have looked forward to another ten to twenty years of life with her children and grandchildren.

As it was, all she could look forward to was being stripped naked, having her head shaved and being left in an unheated room until she was gassed.[316]

*

The following is a description of the final moments in the gas chamber:

"The gassing was a short moment in Auschwitz. As soon as the victims were trapped in the 'shower-room' they recognized in a flash the whole pattern of the destruction process. The imitation shower facilities did not work. Outside, a central switch was thrown to turn off the lights. A Red Cross car drove up with the Cyclon gas, and a masked SS man lifted the glass shutters over the lattice, emptying one can after another into the gas-chamber. The political chief of the camp stood ready with a stop watch in hand.

As the first pellets sublimated on the floor of the chamber, the law of the jungle took over. To escape from the rapidly rising gas, the stronger knocked down the weaker, stepping on the prostrate victims in order to prolong their own life by reaching the gas-free layers of air. The agony lasted for about two minutes, the dying slumping over. Within four minutes everybody in the chamber was dead."[317]

---

[315]   Bideman, Abraham. Op.cit. footnote 311, p. 204.
[316]   Gilbert, Martin. Op.cit. footnote 302, pp. 650-653.

A dry account but more terrible because it is so matter-of-fact.

*

There is an eye-witness account of Convoy 71's arrival at Birkenau from a survivor, Edith Klebender:[318]

"On our arrival at the station of Birkenau on the 15 April 1944 in the evening, we descended from the wagons. An SS asked if amongst the people present there was someone who spoke both French and German. I nominated myself as, being Austrian and living in France, I spoke both languages.

The SS wanted to question the females about their age and particularly those in the last three wagons. I then interpreted and asked the females in the three last wagons what their age was. Then I realized that in the last wagon was a group of 30 children, accompanied by some adults. The children were not with their families but with a group of people accompanying them.

The SS wanted to question the accompanying people whether they were the parents of the children. They replied "No, but we have become their adoptive mothers". I translated this phrase into German and the SS asked me to question the women whether they wished to stay with the children. I asked the question "Do you want to stay with the children?" They replied "Of course". The SS then told the children to get into the trucks, saying "You will arrive very soon". They all climbed into the trucks and I never saw them again."

*

Those selected for work arrived at Auschwitz next day on the 16 April 1944. Photo number 5 on the photo pages shows the main entrance of Auschwitz Camp with the words *Arbeit Macht Frei* over the gate. 165 men were given the numbers 184097 to 184261. The calendar of Auschwitz does not mention any female selections but there must have been some, as in 1945, when the camp was liberated,

---

[317] Hilberg, Raul. The destruction of the European Jews. London, Allen, 1961.
Quoted in Clare, George. Last waltz in Vienna. London, Macmillan, 1981. p.294.
[318] Document provided by the Red Cross International Tracing Service.

91 female survivors of Convoy 71 were counted.[319] Document number 4 on the photo pages gives the basic stark details of Convoy No.71.

Sadly, Hulda Frankenbusch, nee Kerber, was not one of the 91 survivors.

Over 65,000 Jews were deported from Drancy to Auschwitz.[320] This is the story of just one of that number.

The record of their journey is inscribed on the Wall of Names at the Shoah Memorial in Paris and there Hulda's name can be found.[321]

---

[319]  Document provided by the Red Cross International Tracing Service
[320]  United States Holocaust Memorial Museum. Op.cit. footnote 300.
[321]  http://www.memorialdelashoah.org/index.php/en/discovering-the-shoah-memorial/the-wall-of-names/the-wall-of-names. Accessed 25 May 2013.

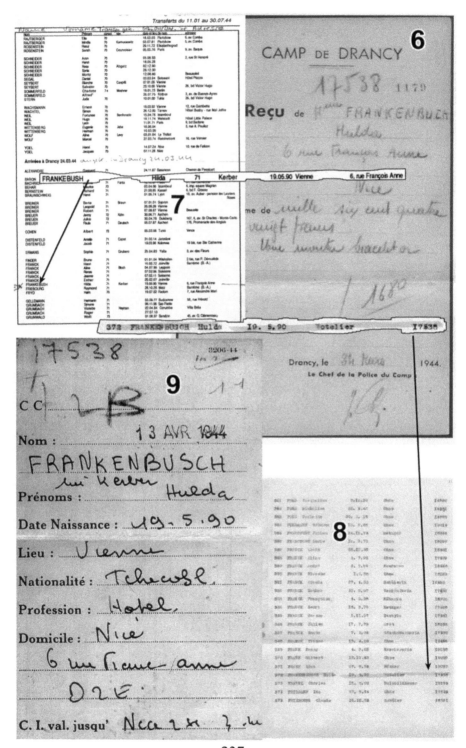

# Epilogue

In May 1944 Ilse and Frank moved to Glasgow and Ilse found work as a clerk. She sent a telegram to Hulda to let her know what they were doing and it was in answer to this telegram, which was forwarded on to the Reverend Gothie, that she learnt of her mother's arrest by the Gestapo.

Frank and Ilse lived at 45 Gamrie Road, Nitshill, Glasgow for a year until the end of April 1945. After that she/they moved to 1371 Barrhead Road, Nitshill Glasgow and Ilse's last communication from that address was dated 16 July 1945.

By this time the war in Europe was over and presumably Ilse had said goodbye to Frank and he'd returned to his family in Holland as expected. Ilse must then have moved back to the south of England as family oral history has her joining the ATS and becoming a driver for an army officer.

Shortly after this she must have met Sydney Waterfall. He was a returned POW and was based at a 'Rest and Recreation' camp near Colchester awaiting demob. Family gossip has it that Ilse saw him there in the swimming pool sometime during the summer of 1945, liked what she saw and jumped in on top of him, he apologised profusely and things went on from there. They were married in January 1946 and settled in the Waterfall family home in Yorkshire. It was in 1945, maybe during her time in the ATS, that Ilse became known as "Frankie", presumably a shortened version of her surname. From then on and especially after her marriage, most of her friends knew her as Frankie Waterfall and only her family continued to call her Ilse. Sidney and Ilse's firstborn (me) arrived in November of that year followed, over the next few years by John in January 1948 and Frances in June 1949.

As well as bringing up three children, Ilse used her language skills as a courier for a travel firm and as a private German teacher. Sadly, she decided not to bring her children up bilingually as she was warned that prejudice against German-speakers in a small village would make their life a misery. Thankfully, one of their neighbours, Hilton Robinson, was a German speaker so Ilse had someone nearby with whom she could speak her native language.

239

Once all the children were well into their teens she trained as a beautician and spent many years working part time demonstrating and selling beauty products. She was also an accomplished needlewoman and craftswoman and later in life sold her work at craft fairs throughout Yorkshire. Ilse died on 28 August 1994, aged 78.

For many years Ilse was racked by guilt at not having done more to help her mother and both Frances and I remember the nights when there were screams and sobs coming from our parents' bedroom next to ours and we knew that mum was having another of her nightmares. We later discovered that the nightmares consisted of Ilse standing on the English side of the Channel and her mother, Hulda, standing on the other side begging Ilse to help her.

Ilse was suffering from what became known as 'survivor's guilt', a condition shared by thousands of others across the world who, themselves, had survived while bearing witness to the disappearance and death of individuals and entire families. The survivors were, in the large part, those of the younger generation as it was they who were usually the ones sent to safety first. Whether this was for practical reasons – that they were considered the most resilient and therefore the most likely to survive the upheaval and challenges of resettlement – or whether it was a basic instinct to ensure the survival of the family and the race, is debatable. Probably a mixture of the two and subconscious at that.

\*

Ilse's father, Rudolf, also survived the war but we, his grandchildren only met him once and all I remember is an old man with a bald head and a finger missing on one hand. He died in 1957 aged 80 and I remember mum having to rush off down to Wales where he was living, to organise the funeral.

Anni and Wim in Holland survived the war and family lore has it that Anni went in to hiding after the invasion of Holland and Wim kept her alive for the duration of the war. Their only child, Vera, was born in May 1944, only one month after the death of her grandmother, Hulda. Anni died in 1994, the same year as her sister Ilse.

Hanne, Anni and Ilse's stepsister, also survived the war though very little is known about where she spent the war years. Family oral history has her walking across Europe as the war ended and maybe making her way towards Anni in Holland. She married a Dutchman,

240

Piet Rook and spent the rest of her life in Canada where her two sons and their families still live.

Szerina Kun and her daughter Alice, from the Budapest branch of the extended family, survived the war in England and both ended their lives there in 1964 and 1998 respectively. It is unknown whether Josef Kun, Szerina's husband, who remained in Europe during the war, survived.

Of the Frankenbusch family in Czechoslovakia, more than 20 lost their lives during the war years – the family was practically wiped out. The same can be said of the Hungarian branch of Hulda's extended family.

Alexander (Sani) Torday/Volnay survived the war but his family lost everything they owned in Budapest. Their villa in Abbazzia stayed in family hands and in a letter written by him to Ilse in 1945 he mentions that he is going to base himself there and rebuild his life.

Robert Miskolczy survived his stint in the Sahara and ended his life in Vienna in 1978. It is unknown whether or not he managed to rejoin his wife Hertha in England after the war.

Irma Langes, Roberts sister lived the rest of her life in England and died there in 1986. Her son Hanns-Walter died in 2007 and lived the rest of his life in the same house that he and his mother had moved into on their arrival in London in 1939. He researched and published his family tree which provided a lot of the links that helped us connect the various parts of the Lowenstein-Frankenbusch extended family.

Grete, Roberts other sister, was deported from Drancy with her husband, Arnold Greif, in 1943 and both died in Auschwitz.

The Princess Margarete Boncompagni lived out the rest of her life in the US and died there in 1974.

\*

The Waterfall family continues to grow and Ilse and Sidney now have two great-grandchildren born in the last three years. All Ilse's grandchildren have a great interest in her family history and in the story that emerged with the discovery of the letters in 2004.

The family will ensure that the legacy of the three women, Gisela, Hulda and Ilse will continue and their courage, strength and belief in the future will not be forgotten.

The last letter in this book was writen by Ilse to Sidney while he was away being processed prior to demob. She is now happy, content and pregnant with me.

*"It's a grand day today and guess what I am doing, I am sitting in the grass basking in the sun and, I must say, Junior and I enjoy it very much! The sun is lovely, we both feel great today and we are perfectly happy. We are both longing for Saturday when we three will be together again.*

*I found some violets and they smell lovely. Oh my darling it's Spring, beautiful Spring and I am happy at last!*

*Never in my life, not even when I was home and protected, have I felt so full of the joys of life than now! Won't it be great to walk through the woods, just we two humans, to rest where we want, to laugh and to sing, and to just be happy!"*

# Who's Who

### Adele
Referred to as Aunt Adele Herzel, a friend of Hulda's, possibly related, emigrated from Vienna and to Italy and lived in Fiume with her family.

### Alexander
Also known as Alex or Sani. Alexander Torday, also known as Alexander Volnay, a friend of Hulda's, possibly related. His family originated in Hungary, but he was a journalist and travelled throughout Europe.

### Alice
Alice Foyle, nee Kun. A cousin of Ilse's, born in Hungary but grew up in Vienna and emigrated to England in 1938.

### Anni
Anni Heniger, nee Frankenbusch. Hulda's elder daughter and Ilse's sister. Married to Wim Heniger, a Dutchman.

### Bauer
The Bauers emigrated to London and Ilse worked in the same building as Mr Bauer for a short time.

### Christel
A friend and correspondent of Ilse's who remained in Vienna during the war.

### Christopher
Christopher Foyle, son of Alice Foyle, nee Kun and distant cousin to the author. Christopher provided information about his side of the extended family.

### Elly
Elly Herzel, mother of Frank Herzel and mother in law of Adele Herzel. Emigrated from Vienna to Italy and died in a sanatorium on Lake Garda.

### Else
Else Kriknelt, friend of Hulda's, who emigrated from Vienna to England. Mother to Liesel and Gretl.

## Frances

Frances Elson, nee Waterfall. Sister to the author and younger daughter of Ilse.

## Frank (1)

Frank Herzel, husband of Adele, Hulda's friend. Son of Elly. Emigrated from Vienna to Italy with his wife and mother.

## Frank (2)

Ilse's lover 1942-45. A Dutchman stranded in England at the outbreak of the war whose family remained in Holland for the duration of the war.

## Gisa

Referred to as Aunt Gisa Miskolczy. A cousin of Gisela and mother of Robert, Grete and Irma.

## Gisela

Gisela Kerber nee Lowenstein. Mother of Hulda, grandmother of Ilse and great-grandmother of the author.

## Grete

Grete Miskolczy, sister to Robert and Irma and distant cousin to Hulda.

## Gretl

Gretl Kriknelt, daughter of Else, Hulda's friend. The family emigrated from Vienna to England.

## Hanne

Hanne Rook, nee Frankenbusch. Ilse's stepsister.

## Hansi

Ilse's best friend in Vienna. She emigrated from Vienna to England and worked with Ilse for a short time in Aberdeenshire.

## Hanns

Hanns-Walter Lange, Irma's son who emigrated to London with his mother. A distant cousin of Ilse's.

## Hertha

Hertha Miskolczy, Robert's wife. She emigrated from Vienna to England.

## Hulda

Hulda Frankenbusch. Gisela Kerber's daughter, Ilse's mother and the author's grandmother.

## Ilse

Ilse Waterfall nee Frankenbusch. Hulda's younger daughter, Gisela's granddaughter and the author's mother.

## Irma

Irma Lange, nee Miskolczy. Wife to Walter, sister to Robert and mother to Hanns. Distant cousin to Hulda. She emigrated to London with her son and Ilse lived in their house for a period of time.

## Johani

A friend and correspondent of Hulda's.

## Johanne

Johanne Rook, formerly Frankenbusch, nee Tietze. Rudolof Frankenbusch's second wife and Ilse's stepmother.

## John

John Waterfall. Ilse's son and brother to the author.

## Josef

Josef Kun. Husband to Szerina and father to Alice. Uncle to Ilse and part of the Hungarian extended family. Stayed in Vienna at the beginning of the war then returned to Hungary.

## Julie (1)

Julie Schafer, known as Aunt Julie Schafer. Cousin to Gisela and sister to Aunt Olga Ammergut.

## Julie (2)

Julie Squarenina. Gisa Miskolczy's sister and aunt to Robert, Grete and Irma.

## Kris

Dr and Frau Kris, friends of Hulda's in Paris.

## Leopold

Leopold Squarenina. Known as Poldi. Julie Sqarenina's son and Hulda's distant cousin.

## Liesel

Liesel Kriknelt. Daughter of Hulda's friend Else Kriknelt and sister to Gretl.

## Margaret

Also known as Margarete. Princess Margaret Boncompagni, nee Draper. Hulda's employer, friend and beneficiary. She financed Hulda's life in France as long as it was possible to do so.

## Mia

Mia Kris, daughter to Dr and Frau Kris, Hulda's friends in Paris. Mia emigrated to London and lived in a convent not far from where Ilse was staying.

## Olga

Olga Ammergut. Known as Aunt Olga Ammergut. Sister to Julie Schafer and cousin to Gisela

## Otto

Otto Frankenbusch. Known as Uncle Otto. Younger brother to Rudolf, brother in law to Hulda and Uncle to Ilse.

## The Princess

Also known as Margaret or Margarete. Princess Margaret Boncompagni, nee Draper. Hulda's employer, friend and beneficiary. She financed Hulda's life in France for as long as it was possible to do so.

## Recht

Herr and Frau Recht. Friends of Hulda's in Paris.

## Richard

Richard Foyle. Husband of Alice Kun, Ilse's cousin, and father to Christopher Foyle

## Robert

Robert Miskolczy. Son of Gisa, brother to Irma and Grete. Friend and cousin of Hulda. He emigrated from Vienna to Paris but spent most of the war in Morocco.

## Roman

Roman Rost. Ilse's fiancé until December 1941.

## Rudi

Hansi's fiancé and friend of Roman.

## Rudolf

Rudolf Frankenbusch. Hulda's husband, Ilse's father and the author's grandfather.

## Sani

Also known as Alex. Alexander Torday, also known as Alexander Volnay, a friend of Hulda's, possibly related.

## Sidney

Sidney Waterfall. Ilse's husband and the author's father.

## Sonia

Daughter of Ilse and sister of John and Frances. The author of this book.

## Szerina

Szerina Kun. Husband of Josef and mother of Alice Foyle, nee Kun.

## Vera

Vera Heniger. Daughter of Anni and cousin to Sonia, John and Frances Waterfall.

## Walter

Walter Lange. Husband to Irma and father of Hanns-Walter.

## Wim

Wim Heniger. Husband to Anni and father of Vera.

## Wynn

Mr Wynn of Morgan Bank, Paris. Princess Margaret Boncompagni's banker who advised Hulda and facilitated the transfer of funds from the Princess to Hulda.

*

# Picture Credits

*Frontespieces*
*Hulda's journey 1938-1944.* Artwork by John Waterfall.
*Lowenstein/Frankenbusch family tree.* Art work by John Waterfall.

## Chapter 1

*Nuremburg Law Chart.* Time Money and Blood. A Website about World War II. Classification of Jews. www.timemoneyandblood.com/HTML/posters/german/nuremberg-laws.html .
*Hulda Kerber 1938.* Photo from the Waterfall Collection.
*Political map of Europe 1938.* www.images.wikia.com/althistory/images/8/8a/Europe_September_1938.png.
*Ilse's French entry visa 1938.* Document from the Waterfall Collection.

## Chapter 2

*Austro-HungarianEmpire1914.* www.cartographersguild.com/attachments/finished-maps/784d1189376323-austro-hungarian-empire-before.png .
**Photo Pages.** 12 photos from the Waterfall Collection.

## Chapter 3

*Hotel de Palais Bourbon.* Photo from the Waterfall Collection.
*Hulda's French ID card.* Document from the Waterfall Collection.

## Chapter 4

*Heather, Ilse's granddaughter wearing the dirndl in 2010.* Photo by Duncan Elson.
*Montmartre cafe scene.* Vintage everyday. Color photos of Paris in the summer of 1939 by LIFE photographer William Vandivert. www.vintage.ed/2013/01/wonderful-color-photos-of-paris-in.html .
*Hulda's Paris, October 1938 – March 1940.* Art work by John Waterfall.
*Letter from Gisela to Ilse.* Document from the Waterfall collection.

## Chapter 5

*Invasion of Poland, September 1939.* United States Holocaust Memorial Museum Photo Archives #431. Copyright of United States Holocaust Memorial Museum.
*Letter to Ilse re the aliens Tribunal, October 1938.* Document from the Waterfall Collection.
*Gisela's Christmas postcard to Ilse, December 1939.* Document from the Waterfall Collection.

## Chapter 6

*Hulda's travel permit from the Czech Military Dept, Paris, February 1940.* Document from the Waterfall Collection.
*Hulda's postcard to Ilse on arrival in Nice, March 1940.* Document from the Waterfall Collection.
*Hulda's Nice, March 1940 – March 1944.* Art work by John Waterfall.
*German Invasion of Denmark and Norway.* United States Holocaust Memorial Museum Photo Archives #438. Copyright of United States Holocaust Memorial Museum.

## Chapter 7

*Rotterdam after the German bombing.* United States Holocaust Memorial Museum Photo Archives #5774. Copyright of the United States Holocaust Memorial Museum.

248

*Hulda's letter after the invasion of Holland.* Document from the Waterfall Collection.

*German Invasion of Holland, Belgium and France, 1940.* United States Holocaust Memorial Museum Photo Archives #367. Copyright of United States Holocaust Memorial Museum

*Divided France June 1940-1944* United States Holocaust Memorial Museum Photo Archives No.1637. Copyright United States Holocaust Memorial Museum.

*Roman's letter to Ilse, November 1940.* Document from the Waterfall Collection.

## Chapter 8

*Letter from Hulda to Ilse, February 1941.* Document from the Waterfall Collection.

*Telegram announcing Anni's pregnancy, March 1941.* Document from the Waterfall Collection.

*Letter from the Home Office, July 1941.* Document from the Waterfall Collection.

*Gisela's last letter.* Document from the Waterfall Collection.

## Chapter 9

*Letter to Ilse from the Czech Legation, London, March 1942.* Document from the Waterfall Collection.

*Hulda's telegram to Ilse about Gisela's deportation, April 1942.* Document from the Waterfall Collection.

*Telegram from Denise Grunewald to Ilse concerning Hulda, September 1942.* Document from the Waterfall Collection.

*Letter from Mary Campion, British Red Cross, about Hulda's arrest and release, August 1942.* Document from the Waterfall Collection.

*Birthday telegram to Ilse from Hulda via the Red Cross, November 1942.* Document from the Waterfall Collection.

## Chapter 10

*Telegram from Ilse to Hulda, December 1942.* Document from the Waterfall Collection.

*Letter from the Foreign Office to Ilse, April 1943.* Document from the Waterfall Collection.

*Letter from the Red Cross to Ilse giving news of Hulda, September 1943.* Document from the Waterfall Collection.

*Telegram from Hulda to Ilse, January 1944.* Document from the Waterfall Collection.

*Plaque commemorating Jews deported from Nice railway station, Sept 1943-July 1944.* Photo taken by Duncan Elson.

*Letter from Mlle Moretti to Reverend Gothie about Hulda's arrest by the Gestapo, March 1944.* Document from the Waterfall Collection.

## Chapter 11

*1. Lining up for selection.* United States Holocaust Museum Photo Archives #3132. Copyright of United States Holocaust Museum.

*2. Aerial view of Drancy camp.* United States Holocaust Museum Photo Archives #652. Copyright of United States Holocaust Museum.

*3. Drancy camp.* Jewish Virtual Library. www.jewishvirtuallibrary.org/images/Drancy .

*4. Transport 71 record.* Photo from the Powles Collection.

*5. Main entrance to Auschwitz camp.* United States Holocaust Museum Photo Archives #5174. Copyright of United States Holocaust Museum.
*6. Arrival at Drancy.* Document from the Waterfall Collection.
*7. Register of deportees.* Document from the Waterfall Collection.
*8. Camp diary.* Document from the Waterfall Collection.
*9. Leaving Drancy.* Document from the Waterfall Collection.


*

All images in this book have been enhanced by D.W.Elson of Rothbury.

## Acknowledgements

First it's important to acknowledge the part that my parents played in the production of this book. My mother, Ilse Waterfall nee Frankenbusch treasured the letters from her mother, grandmother and friends and kept them safe until her death in 1994. My father, Sidney Waterfall, knew how precious they were for my mother and continued to keep them safe until his death in 2004. My siblings and I will be forever grateful to have this record of the lives of the three women during the war and we hope that the future generations of the family will appreciate as we do the sacrifices that they and thousands of other made so that we can live comfortably and in peace.

My niece Nicola Waterfall took on the unenviable job of sorting through the letters and organising, preserving, copying and storing them. She is the person who continues to research and build the family tree. My brother, John Waterfall, assists with the production of the on-line version of the family tree and produced the Lowenstein – Frankenbusch family tree that is the Frontespiece of the book. He also produced the two maps of Paris and Nice and helped with the proof-reading. My sister, Frances Elson, continually encouraged me to keep going and listened patiently to my endless moans and groans. She also helped considerably with the proof-reading and publicising of the book amongst family, friends and acquaintances. It's probably due to Fran's enthusiasm for the project that the book finally got finished.

Thanks must also go to my cousins, Vera Heniger in Holland and Christopher Foyle in Monaco who both provided valuable pieces of information about their branches of the extended family.

My biggest thanks are to my brother-in-law, Duncan Elson and to my translators.

Duncan, a professional photographer, used his skills to make the photos and other images in the book as clear and sharp as they are. He is also a computer whizz and it was he who edited and then produced the published version. He dealt with my nit-picking demands with endless patience and there must have been many times when he wondered just what he'd let himself in for.

The translators, Birgit Nielsen, Janine Hogben, Angela Lyons, Helen Powles and Gemma Kennedy all worked unpaid because they were interested in the story and wanted to see the book brought to

251

fruition. Between them they translated over 120 documents in their spare time and between their day jobs and family lives. Helen also helped by providing some of the images used in the book.

Peter Walton in Darwin, Australia set me on the right track where style, format, referencing and content were concerned.

Thank goodness for Google by which means I found Wikipedia and the website for the United States Holocaust Memorial Museum, both of which provided invaluable information.

Last, but not least, I have to thank my partner, Vaina Ioane, for his patience with, and toleration of, my obsession. He lived with the book for five years and he's probably very relieved that it's now finished.

Lightning Source UK Ltd.
Milton Keynes UK
UKHW011828040719

345589UK00001B/162/P